Recovering from the Recovery:
A Recipe for Survival

By Anil B. Bhatt

Changing our behavior to avoid future crises

Open Door Publications, LLC

Recovering from the Recovery
A Recipe for Survival

ISBN: 978-0-9960985-1-9

Printed in the United States

Published by
Open Door Publications
2113 Stackhouse Dr.
Yardley, PA 19067

Cover Design by Chameleon Studios, LLC

www.OpenDoorPublications.com

Praise for *Recovery from the Recovery: A Simple Recipe*

Recovering from the Recovery is much more than a book of financial advice. With cutting insight borne of his vast experience in business and accounting, Anil Bhatt writes with wisdom and compassion and draws the reader into his ethical, optimistic worldview. As a psychiatrist, I am deeply familiar with how we can let our emotions and limited perspective affect our good judgment. Few thinkers can elevate this perspective to embrace the concerns of the society and world at large. Somehow, Bhatt has managed to gently and powerfully guide us towards a global vision of responsibility, morals, and ultimately, success and satisfaction for all. Read this book, and share it with your friends and family.

Joseph Salvatore MD,
Psychiatrist, Princeton, New Jersey

Anil Bhatt brings a compassionate heart and the three decades of practitioner insights to this very readable analysis of the financial crisis.

Julia Sass Rubin,
Associate Professor, Rutgers University

To my late Parents
Mr. B. M. Bhatt and Mrs. I. B. Bhatt
for their tireless efforts in changing
many lives

Table of Contents

Introduction

The financial crisis of 2008 was an eye opener. In the aftermath, millions lost their jobs, homes, and nest eggs through no fault of theirs. They felt helpless because they did not have the requisite knowledge and understanding of the risks associated with home ownership and investing in financial instruments. As human history has witnessed, we normally move from one crisis to another without learning enough, leaving us unprepared to deal with the future. We manage to elude the ultimate wisdom of making this world free of human suffering. We make great strides and progress in times of peace, but have not been able to fully achieve human freedom, peace, and harmony among peoples of all races, nationalities, and religions, as evident from man-made disasters such as the financial crisis.

In order to understand and learn from such crises, we must take a holistic approach and go beyond the events themselves and delve into our daily lives to reflect on what makes us prone to these types of dangers in the first place.

♦♦♦

I am a public accountant blessed with a wonderful wife, two adult children, a very close family, and countless friends and colleagues. In 2006, after working as an accountant for 30 years, I decided to take a sabbatical. In the ensuing months I began some serious soul searching to figure out my next move. I wanted to serve independently with a social purpose where I would not be forced to compromise the principles I believed in deeply. Two years later, while still undecided about my future, the United States had its worst economic crisis, as well as the most intensely fought Democratic primaries of our generation. Based on my wife's advice, I decided to rejoin the profession of accountancy, but on my own terms, as my own boss taking on all of the associated responsibilities, obligations, and risks.

It has been an interesting and challenging journey. Most of my experiences hold true for all Americans. During these challenging economic times, some people are holding multiple jobs just to keep afloat. Others have had to put their dreams of retirement on hold and instead start new careers in their 70s and 80s. New graduates are unable to find suitable jobs in their dream careers. And the sad saga continues.

There are many unanswered questions. In the last few years, I tried to find answers not only to the causes and effects of the crisis itself, but also the factors outside of the financial arena. These factors include: our way of life, our social ways and beliefs, our political and our religious preferences. As important as it is to overcome these enormous challenges for our generation and get back on track, the big question is: What do we have to offer to future generations in terms of basic human rights and decent living conditions to sustain them into the next century? Together our collective wisdom and personal sacrifices will see us through these trying times into a brighter future.

As we muddle through these tough economic times, we need to become socially conscious of our surroundings. These discussions can start either at a local coffeehouse or a church gathering, but they need to make it into our daily routine and into every aspect of our lives. Our obsession with financial and economic success distracts us from our fundamental obligation toward human freedom and the rights of those who are less fortunate.

Even though it may seem that we have graduated from being stone-age beasts to civilized human beings, in reality we only managed to build boundaries, barriers, and empires by breaking the world apart in the process. We passed along our imperfectness, biases, and indifferences to the next generation. There is this disconnect between what students are taught in school versus the real world they face upon graduation. The cycle seems to perpetuate itself throughout the generations.

The views I held before the crisis became even stronger, and I have learned there are many who share my feelings and frustrations. This book is a continuation of my coffeehouse conversations, but with a sense of urgency and a debate about finding ways to correct our errors and pave a smooth path as we build "our field of dreams" toward prosperity.

Most of the world is also facing and dealing with these same issues without much success. The financial crisis was global. It acted much like a tsunami, destroying everything in its path. Europe and the Middle East are facing fiscal and political uncertainties. A new political, economic, and social order is lurking on the horizon and making its presence felt in no uncertain terms. Are we, the people of the free world, up to that task of relinquishing the past, cleansing ourselves of the wounds, and forging ahead with renewed vigor and optimism?

Keeping in mind the timeless teachings of Christ, Buddha, and great souls such as Gandhi, one needs to dig deep into one's mind and soul to find answers to help one succeed. Buddha's life and teachings tell us to look beyond our troubles, and away from our material surroundings, and rather turn to nature, trees, ocean, sky, and the interaction of all natural forces to seek answers. That is where I am seeking answers to my puzzles, and that is where I hope to meet you in a common quest for justice and prosperity for all because there is a permanency in nature, not found in man-made creations.

As elected government officials, in consultation with experts, try to find solutions to the underlying economic problems and steer us toward prosperity, common citizens need to cooperate in the process of recovery and try to live their lives as sensibly as possible. As responsible citizens we have to be alert and proactive and make sure our voices are heard, not buried at the back of newspapers and magazines, in the op-ed section.

Prior to this financial crisis, we sailed merrily along praising the benefits of globalization. After the crisis, though, we have retreated, and our policies tend to be more protectionist. That is a mistake. Thomas Friedman's book, *The World Is Flat,* is worth revisiting in that regard. He lists the forces that are responsible for flattening the world, among them the fall of Berlin Wall on November 9, 1989, which resulted in the formation of the European Union; outsourcing of functions; creating efficiencies at home and opportunities abroad for those who service them; offshoring of operations to reduce costs by use of cheap labor; taxes and subsidized energy and lower healthcare costs in a host country; insourcing by creating value horizontally; and in-forming, which is the ability to use technology through universal access to inform oneself. He observes those opposed to outsourcing assume everything that is going to be invented has been invented, and therefore economic competition is a zero-sum game. This is not true as more skilled jobs are created elsewhere, so are cost efficiencies.

The next generation is comfortable operating in this new flat world. Unfortunately the severity of the current economic condition and the aftereffects caused by the crisis may not seem that obvious to them. Unless we narrate our struggles and our efforts to deal with the crisis and pave a clear path for the future, the next generation will never forgive us. The time has come to establish a new order. This can be achieved only by stepping outside of our comfort zones and not being overly concerned about our own material well-being. In the new future, our success will not only be measured in financial terms, but also by the social footprint we leave behind.

As concluded by the Financial Crisis Inquiry Commission (FCIC) created by Congress and the President, "the crisis was avoidable—a result of human actions, inactions, and misjudgments. The greatest tragedy would be to accept the refrain that no one could have seen this coming, and thus nothing could have been done. If we accept this notion, it will happen again." From the study of the Commission's report, it becomes clear our financial systems, our business practices, our lack of effective controls and oversight, and our obsession with home ownership without regard to affordability, all contributed to the meltdown. Many Americans have learned that owning a home is a luxury they cannot afford. For those young adults who believed home ownership was an "inalienable right," it is hard to accept, but a reality they cannot afford to ignore. Tomorrow's leaders need to set their own standards and create their own recipe for success and sustainability. We can provide some guidance as the financial disaster is still fresh and we are still learning about its underlying causes.

Even though "this time is no different than the previous times," and the financial crisis could have been averted if we had the right controls in place and working, the current crisis created an opportunity to look at it from a fresh perspective, to revamp our old systems and not return to the old norms. That would certainly be a recipe for another disaster.

We must understand what caused the crisis. Who were the players? What were the consequences of the crisis? How did the government intervene to avoid a total meltdown? It is equally important to reflect on our own behavior as well as how we interact with one another. We need to look into the causes of poverty and wars, and how religion, class warfare, and education all affect our lives. We need to understand the roles of the people, businesses, governments and their agencies, not-for-profit organizations, multilateral global organizations, and nongovernmental organizations. The discussion cannot be complete without evaluating our assets, our natural resources, as well as identifying our liabilities, how to achieve sustainability, and defining and fulfilling our moral and social obligations. For it is this holistic approach that will enable us to deal with any crisis, however huge and insurmountable it may seem.

Part I:

The Crisis & the Aftermath:
Our People
Our Institutions
Our Shortcomings

Chapter 1
The Financial Crisis of 2008

If money is all that a man makes, then he will be poor; poor in happiness, and poor in all that makes life worth living.

Herbert N. Casson
Canadian Journalist & Author

Our 2008 summer vacation was memorable. My wife and I drove 4,200 miles coast to coast from New Jersey to Seattle, stopping along the way in Washington, D.C.; Charleston, West Virginia; St. Louis, Missouri; Omaha, Nebraska; Denver, Colorado; Salt Lake City, Utah; and Yellowstone National Park in Wyoming. It is impossible to capture a full perspective of the United States in only 12 to 13 days, but we were able to get a glimpse of it through our cameras that will remain etched in our memories forever. As we found out, perhaps the best way to travel in a country as vast and diverse as ours is by car; horseback would have been even better, but unfortunately we had neither the patience nor the skills for that.

The vacation was followed by a hot summer and the nail-biting primaries. Just as 2008 was about to close its doors, we were hit with one of the worst financial crises in our nation's history. Within days the Dow Jones Industrial Average, a benchmark indicator of market activity, plunged more than 700 points, and lost approximately half of its value that year. This sudden and huge drop in the stock market created panic among the investors, who lost faith in the system. This was not an isolated phenomenon; it was triggered by a collapse in the housing industry.

The government immediately intervened by infusing funds to resuscitate the economy. For years to come, people and businesses will have to work very hard and make necessary sacrifices, while the government will have to implement effective national fiscal policies and trade agreements with our partners in the world to ease the global effect of the crisis as well.

The aftermath of the crisis created a deep recession evidenced by high unemployment, an economic slump, and credit squeeze, all of which further weakened manufacturing, housing, and related industries. Since these sectors are mutually dependent, the crisis in one area created a domino effect in the other, bringing about an overall fallout.

How it all started

The financial crisis did not happen in an instant. Like hot lava, it percolated for a long time. It was the result of many wrong things happening over a period of years, unchecked, undetected, and untreated. It was like a cancer spreading through our entire system.

According to the prognosis of the Financial Crisis Inquiry Commission in its report:

1. This financial crisis was avoidable.

2. Widespread failures in financial regulation and supervision proved devastating to the stability of the nation's financial markets.

3. Dramatic failures of corporate governance and risk management at many systemically important financial institutions were a key cause of this crisis.

4. A combination of excessive borrowing, risky investments, and lack of transparency put the financial system on a collision course with the crisis.

5. The government was ill-prepared for the crisis, and its inconsistent response added to the uncertainty and panic in the financial markets.

6. There was a systemic breakdown in accountability and ethics.

7. The collapsing mortgage-lending standards and the mortgage securitization pipeline lit and spread the flame of contagion and crisis.

8. Over-the–counter derivatives contributed significantly to this crisis.

9. The failures of credit rating agencies were essential cogs in the wheel of financial destruction.

In some measure, we are all to blame for this colossal crisis. The Financial Crisis Inquiry Commission aptly quoted Cassius who says in Shakespeare's *Julius Caesar*, "the fault…is not in our stars, but in ourselves." When we wake up every morning we need to remind ourselves of that statement and plan our day in such a way that we do our share of good to prevent such man-made disasters from happening again.

What went wrong?

One of the key elements of the current crisis was the lending practices associated with home ownership. As has since been made public, there was a widespread practice of loans being made without adequate paperwork, with light background checks on income verifications, and without adequate disclosures, called "truth in lending." Sub-prime loans were made to many borrowers with bad credit histories of low income and low credit scores. All of this happened without adequate controls and oversight. As borrowing for homes became easier, more people bought real estate without regard to future affordability. Some were lured into taking out mortgages at low teaser rates, which would rise. The demand for housing skyrocketed as did market values. The housing bubble grew larger by the day. Everybody was riding on this bubble. The financial industry, which invested very heavily in mortgages and mortgage-backed securities, had a lot at stake in the event of a system-wide failure. That is exactly what happened when borrowers could not pay their new, higher mortgages and overnight these loans became delinquent. All those who carried these mortgages on their books, and the investors who lent billions of dollars against those mortgages, ran for cover and quickly found there was no place to hide. The exposures created shockwaves around the entire world. The financial institutions that borrowed against the mortgage-backed securities could not pay their bond calls and interest. Some of these institutions failed for lack of liquidity. The crisis was exacerbated by the widespread risk and high leverage prevalent among trading in certain complex financial instruments called derivatives, which are instruments whose values are derived from other negotiable financial instruments, such as stocks.

As the housing market started its downward slide, people who owed more than the value of their homes became delinquent. Running out of options, many had to foreclose on their properties. The financial, auto, manufacturing, and housing industries lost millions of jobs, which made matters worse, as those otherwise solvent homeowners could no longer afford their mortgages without their paychecks.

We may analyze the crisis all we want, and study closely all the factors and players who contributed to it, but the truth is, we all failed because we acted irresponsibly, selfishly, and insensibly. We swerved from our moral and social compass. Unless we clean up our act and think and behave as responsible human beings, we could end up in a big mess again. Who would bail us out then?

One of the drawbacks of a capitalistic structure is, while promoting individual growth and expansion, it also leaves many behind. It is this disconnect between those with plenty and the disadvantaged masses that serves as a fertile ground for a crisis such as this to take root. We created a selfish and unethical culture which corrupted our social and economic systems, and allowed some of the individual financial scandals to flourish. For example, the Ponzi scheme employed by Bernard Madoff, that came to surface in late 2008, as well as the Enron scandal in the late 1990s and early 2000. Madoff had been scheming for more than a decade before it became public in late 2008. At that time he disclosed the facts of his scheme to his sons, who were working with him in his security trading business. He posed as an investment advisor and broker and conned people into investing in his company. No money was ever invested in any securities. Fictitious monthly statements were sent to the clients listing trades, income, and portfolio position at the end of the period—none of it was real. The Enron scandal was a skillfully orchestrated accounting manipulation that ill-benefited the key employees and players financially. This individual greed also pervaded through our whole financial system, which suffered from lack of controls, oversight, breaches of trust, and a disregarding of rules and laws. This systemic failure affected everyone because of the interconnectedness of various segments of the economy. It broke down all economic and financial systems and institutions.

There is a lot to learn from the crisis and the profound effect it is has had on all of us. Some people may never recover. Some questions may never be answered. Frank Partnoy, a professor of law and finance at the University of San Diego, explains our role as individuals and investors, and the impact our actions can have on our own financial fortunes. In the epilogue to his book, *Infectious Greed*, Partnoy states "today there are an astonishing number of individuals buying and selling stocks. Maybe you are one of them. Maybe you contributed to the volatile and risky nature of these new markets. As you reflect on the story of the last twenty years of risk and deceit, ask yourself: did I carefully read the annual reports of the companies whose stock I bought? Did I really understand what those companies were doing, who their customers were and how they made money? Did I know how much they were involved in complex financial instruments? Did I resist the recommendations of friends, colleagues, and talking heads on television about the latest hot stock? If you answered NO, then you have one more person to blame, in addition to the accountants, bankers, lawyers, credit raters, corporate executives, directors and regulators who failed to spot the various financial schemes of recent years, YOU." As responsible citizens, we have the choice to take the often-travelled road (with its pitfalls) or the path of the righteous.

How about the millions of people who have neither the requisite knowledge nor the experience and education to decide what's good for them? Their actions may have unintended social and economic consequences, both for themselves and for society at large. That's where accountants, lawyers, teachers, financial advisors, regulators, and the government step in to provide the necessary guidance. We will all have to forgo some profits and divert them for the betterment of the community.

In these rebuilding efforts we need to thank social activists already working in our communities, making personal sacrifices, providing food, clothing, education, and legal help to the poor while helping to create a positive self-image among the underprivileged or handicapped youth and adults alike. For many on the margins of destitution, life is a daily struggle. It is not a one-time event or disaster. They do not need a financial education because they do not have a spare dollar to invest. America was once thought of as a land of opportunity where everyone could make it. Today that prophecy is unrealistic for many.

What the crisis meant to Main Street

Simply speaking, for most of "Main Street America" the crisis has meant:

- Loss of job, promotion and/or a raise.
- Loss of home, or equity in the home and consequent inability to meet the home costs.
- Loss in value of retirement accounts, potentially significantly depending on allocation of investments.
- Inability to repay student loans and unaffordable

tuition for higher education.
- Unexpected relocation costs for those with dim prospects of finding suitable jobs in their present location.
- Additional medical benefit costs for those displaced from their jobs.
- Indefinite delay in many plans and prospects for the future.
- Unavoidable separation from families and loved ones for economic reasons.

In addition, people faced psychological battles brought on by their financial inadequacy. Not all are strong enough to withstand these pressures; as a result many break down. There are not enough crisis centers that can help people deal with their economic, financial, and social difficulties. This is covered in detail in Chapter 4.

What the crisis meant to Wall Street

The 2008 crisis brought as much misery to Wall Street as it brought to Main Street. Here is a list:

- Post crisis, Wall Street lost hundreds of thousands of jobs. Since 2008, some of those jobs have been reinstated as the financial firms have turned the corner to embrace "profitability" again.
- The systemic failure brought down Merrill Lynch (which was acquired by Bank of

America), Bear Stearns, and Lehman Brothers. AIG, an insurance giant, was bailed out by the government and Wall Street giants.

- Government, which bailed out the firms by infusing $700 billion of TARP (Troubled Asset Relief Program), among other government commitments, had an equity stake and a say in governance. (As of 2013 these funds had been repaid with interest.)
- In 2010, the government passed the Dodd-Frank Wall Street Reform and Consumer Protection Act (Dodd-Frank Act). It is designed to put restrictions on certain trading activities of financial firms so it can lower the systemic risks to the financial system and protect the consumers. As anticipated, there is a widespread opposition to certain rules and provisions in the Act, from the financial sector.

Under the Dodd-Frank Act, the Securities and Exchange Commission (SEC) and the Commodity Futures Trading Commission (CFTC) were given wide powers to control hedge funds and similar activities, which previously enjoyed relaxed regulation. The problems these regulatory agencies and even the Internal Revenue Service face is the lack of resources in terms of adequate manpower and budgets necessary for effective implementation. That is the very reason why this "catch me if you can" mentality has prevailed among our nation's institutions and individual private citizens for this long.

There has been a growing concern among the economic community and regulators that the Dodd-Frank Act did not adequately deal with Too-Big-To-Fail banks as shared by Neil Barofsky, in his book *Bailout*. He was the Special Inspector General for the TARP. He further states "the 848 plus page long act in many ways is too big to succeed." One must not be surprised when something is put out by the 'Washington Machine,' for example, our Internal Revenue Code, which is thousands of pages long and keeps growing every time there is an attempt to simplify it. Maybe we need only Ten Commandments to bring us all to our senses, just as in biblical times.

It was painful for Neil Barofsky and his team, who were responsible for overseeing the TARP program, to find out that the very institutions which were entrusted with the TARP money to resuscitate the market did not hesitate to make misrepresentations, to cough out additional TARP funds. Further, it could not have been easy for them to see that AIG, an insurance giant which was bailed out by hundreds of billions of taxpayers' money, requested $168 million from those funds to be used for retention bonuses to employees in its financial product division. In 2010 alone, compensation for the top 25 Wall Street firms broke records at $135 billion. All this at a time when Main Street saw a loss of millions of jobs, no raises or bonuses for those who were lucky enough to hold onto their jobs, losses in retirement accounts, home values, and bleak prospect of home foreclosures.

In essence, we feel sorry for those who have lost their wealth and hard earned savings and livelihoods for no fault of theirs, but we do not feel sorry for those who had a free ride for way too long. Can there be equity for those who created the "inequality" in the first place?

Six years into the crisis, the nation's leading economists, pundits, and notables in academia are still skeptical about the direction in which we are headed: definitely not toward an intended path of financial and fiscal discipline. The infusion of federal funds into the financial sector and other essential industries should only be utilized for growth and providing badly needed working capital to existing and emerging businesses. They should not be diverted to investing in complex financial instruments and toxic assets. Judging from the daily newspaper reporting, the uncontained risk taking associated with trading still prevails so as sub-prime lending in auto loans and major financial institutions are continuing to pay billions of dollars in fees and penalties to settle the cases, some originated during the crisis. It makes you wonder whether these behemoth institutions have learned their lessons or will seek protection again if needed to, under the too-big-to-fail theory.

Any reform, and especially the one dealing with our financial system, cannot accomplish its goal by only focusing on the cures (with their inherent dangers and limitations) to remedy the current situation, but by finding and implementing the long term solutions that can *prevent* such man-made disasters from happening again.

Role of the Financial Crisis Inquiry Commission

The Federal Crisis Inquiry Commission (FCIC) was an independent 10-member commission consisting of private citizens with extensive experience in housing, economics, finance, market regulation, banking, and consumer protection. Six members were appointed by the Democrats in Congress, and four by Republicans. The Commission, with the assistance of its staff, reviewed millions of documents, interviewed hundreds of witnesses, and held weeks of public hearings across the country before arriving at their conclusions.

Although the Commission was refrained from making any policy recommendations, after an extensive and thorough study of documents and hearing testimonies of people who were directly affected by the crisis and those working with various institutions and agencies, it made these several substantive conclusions:

- The system was flooded with risky mortgages. There were widespread, lax lending practices, and lack of proper oversight.
- The relaxed monetary policy of the Federal Reserve and flow of sovereign funds created the

housing bubble starting as early as the 1990s when the Administration initiated the measures that made home ownership affordable and the process less cumbersome. These practices would continue for nearly two decades, all the way up to the point when the housing bubble burst.

- The investments into mortgages and mortgage-backed securities were made based on credit ratings, but the rating agencies were not adequately regulated by the Securities and Exchange Commission (SEC). Further, the rating agencies' ratings were based on flawed and outmoded models.
- The creation of Collateralized Debt Obligations (CDO) composed of the riskier tranches or strata of the underlying mortgages fueled demand for non-prime mortgage securitization (loans were converted into marketable securities) and contributed to the housing bubble. Simultaneously, instruments such as credit default swaps were created to hedge for or against mortgage defaults. Many systemically large institutions carried these assets on their books, which contributed to huge losses when these assets were deemed toxic.
- Investors were not informed, or were misled, about the poor quality of the mortgages contained in the mortgage related securities.
- The business model under which firms issuing securities paid for their ratings seriously

undermined the quality and integrity of those ratings. The rating agencies placed market share and profit considerations above the quality and integrity of their rating.

- High leverage, inadequate capital, and short term funding made many financial institutions extraordinarily vulnerable to the downturn in the market in 2007. Investment banks had leverage ratios of as high as 40 to 1, meaning for every $40 of assets, there was only $1 in capital. Fannie Mae and Freddie Mac, government sponsored entities, guaranteed the majority of mortgages in this country, had even higher leverage ratios, up to 75 to 1. The financial statements of most of the financial institutions never fully reported the loss exposure on these toxic assets. Many had to restate both the earnings estimates they gave to Wall Street as well as the issued statements.
- Bear Stearns, a major firm with excessive hedge fund activity, and AIG, an insurance giant whose financial products had significant sub-prime exposure, were affected by the collapse of the housing bubble first, creating financial pressures on their parent companies.
- The losses in sub-prime mortgage market at large firms such as Merrill Lynch, Citigroup, and AIG were due to failure in corporate governance and risk management. Executive compensation at large firms was tied into short term risk taking, putting further drain on their

cash flows and their ability to sustain.

- There was a widespread belief that regulation was unduly burdensome, the financial institutions were capable of self-regulation, and that regulators should not interfere with activities reported as profitable. As it became clearer later, the overexposure to risky mortgage assets was subject to runs by creditors and depositors.
- Deregulation of Over–the-Counter (OTC) derivatives, including credit default swaps, effectively eliminated federal and state regulation of these products including capital and margin requirements. The AIG insurance company was so interconnected with many large commercial banks, investment banks, and other financial institutions through counterparty credit relationships on credit default swaps and other activities such as securities lending that its potential failure created systemic risk. AIG's existence was deemed "too big to fail," and the government committed $180 billion to its rescue. The move was believed to have stopped the bleeding, which, if untreated, would have brought a complete meltdown of the country's financial system.
- As many financial institutions failed, panic gripped the market, the credit market seized up, and the stock market plunged. As a result of the financial meltdown, many firms either failed or merged during the crisis, creating the US

financial sector more concentrated than ever in the hands of a few very large systemically important institutions. As a result this concentration places greater responsibility on regulators for effective oversight of these institutions.

As narrated by the FCIC through its interviews and hearings, we become aware of the countless homeowners who had to sell their homes in order to take care of expenses such as medical care for their loved ones, starting new businesses, and relocating to find a decent job someplace else. Some sold their homes as a short sale, which means for less than the balance of the mortgage. In Arizona, California, Florida, Michigan, and Nevada, and other places, some mortgage holders found themselves owing more than their homes were worth.

Based on the fact there is very little improvement in many areas of the economy that were badly hit by the crisis, it is obvious either we have not found all the solutions or we lack in our efforts to bring about the changes necessary for a turnaround. Our youth today need to have adequate financial knowledge to make intelligent and responsible decisions on their own. Part of the long term solution would be including the study and practice of accounting, basic economics, and ethics into our core curriculum. This interdisciplinary and holistic approach in our education system would help mold our nation's future and make us better equipped to cope with the challenges ahead. The other area of importance is the inclusion of international study in higher education, through which our youth can better understand the problems and challenges being faced around the globe. Our challenge is not only to understand the current crisis, but also to study and be aware of the many factors found common during the "Eight Centuries of Financial Folly," as aptly captured by Carmen M. Reinhart and Kenneth S. Rogoff in their 2009 book, *This Time Is Different*. Reinhart and Rogoff analyzed the prior crises using quantitative data including domestic and foreign debt, prices, exchange rates, currency debasement, inflation, and gross domestic product measures. Then they plotted the interrelationships of these factors on a time scale. Using an empirical approach, they explained the effect of these factors leading up to each crisis, including the current one. In order to fully understand a phenomenon of this nature, one must understand both the quantitative as well as non-quantitative factors.

The following are some of their observations and explanations of the current crisis and comparisons to past episodes the authors made. They concluded that the current crisis is no different than the previous crises.

- The housing price declines during the current crisis were as severe as in 1929 with average price declines over even a longer period.
- The equity price declines were also significant just as in prior crises. Although the bounce back

in equity prices is on track as on previous occasions, the housing market is still lagging because the unemployment rate is still high, the new stricter regulatory standards have made the home ownership process cumbersome, and up until now there was low inflow of foreign investment.

- The data suggest a buildup in government debt has been a defining characteristic of the aftermath of banking crises evidently because of reduction in revenue, and deep recession in the ensuing period.
- The authors further observed that for banking crises, real housing prices are nearly at the top of the list of reliable indicators, surpassing the current balances and real stock prices.
- They also observed the banking crises tend to be protracted affairs, meaning they are extended and stretched by the authorities by their denial, governments suffering from reduction in revenues, and bailout costs.
- The authors further concluded financial crises seldom occur in a vacuum; they are hardly isolated episodes.

Now that we understand what caused the crisis, and the economic indicators that gave the warning signals, and we have seen what follows that crisis, our task is to understand the roles various organizations including private citizens can play in repairing the damage, and more importantly, create a strong financial and economic environment that will enable us to prevent future financial crises from happening.

Here is a simple *plan of action* that the private citizens can follow in dealing with their day to day finances:

- Build your team of experts such as accountants, attorneys, and financial advisors who you can trust and who can guide you through the intricacy of the financial and legal process of business dealings in a language you can understand.
- Self-educate in home economics and finances by reading newspapers, business weeklies, books, and the internet to become familiar with the jargon so you can communicate with your trusted advisors intelligently and efficiently.
- Use a common sense approach in dealing with financial issues, and look for parallels in life to relate them to your situation. Follow the lead of financial gurus such as Warren Buffett in this area.
- Remain proactive and get involved with the decision making in weighing options whether to buy, sell, and why? Study the companies and the industry they are in before investing in them. Have a long term perspective. Again, remember Mr. Buffet's favorite line, "You cannot expect to have a baby in one month by making nine women pregnant."
- Stay current with the policies, politics, and legislation that affect your life, and actively pursue

avenues to facilitate change. Build alliances to promote change that improves communities.

- Be flexible and realistic in choosing jobs and careers because sometimes you may have to take detours to reach your destination, especially in today's tough economic environment.
- Appoint a mentor or a coach to guide you through the path of recovery. (I chose my wife because she has always displayed an unbiased and balanced approach to life and possess a rare ability to see through common problems day in and day out.)

Beware. In spite of all our individual efforts on Main Street to bring our house in order, there is always that danger lurking in the distance, a build-up of another "financial storm," because the air is not as clear yet, and the skies are not as blue as we would like, and we get this strange feeling that we are sitting on a wide *fault line* that could rupture any moment and take down everything. If only so we can stop it from happening again!

CHAPTER 2
The Role of Organizations

We are rich only through what we give, and poor only through what we refuse.

Anne-Sophie Swetchine
Russian-French Writer

We live in an interconnected society. Our actions have consequences that not only affect us, but also those around us and even those remotely connected to us. We are called upon to play many roles, some of which may create a conflict and require our judgment when acting in those multiple roles. As a professional, I wrestle with the challenges of multiple roles. In order to fully understand the causes of the current crisis and find ways to prevent it from happening again, it is important to understand the many roles of all the players:

- We the People
- Our Heroes
- Our Leaders
- Businesses
- Professionals
- Governments
- Nongovernmental Organizations
- Nonprofit Organizations & Educational Institutions
- Multilateral organizations
- Trade Associations
- Lobbying Groups

The following is a brief description of these respective roles.

We the People

We are the lifeblood and the constituent parts of our society. We are both the contributors to, as well as the beneficiaries of our social and economic systems. We have multiple roles. We raise families and form organizations, corporations, and institutions. We are therefore regarded as human capital that creates and grows business capital. In order to carry out these multiple tasks, we need to be mentally strong and must have the requisite education, knowledge, and experience to succeed in all these tasks. As an integral part of the organizations we belong to, we need to understand the distinction between our roles as individuals versus our roles as stewards of the organizations we represent.

In order to achieve and maintain that delicate balance, there needs to be government rules, regulations, and bylaws to guide us, as well as moral laws to conduct as responsible individuals of the society. Our success as a society depends on these two pillars working together. As the architects of our local, national, and international systems, we have a collective responsibility to ensure our governments and institutions function efficiently and carry out their intended purposes. If we fail in this obligation, the success of our governments and institutions will never be guaranteed. Our responsibility does not end with casting our votes; that is where it starts. Let your voices be heard, and your values be counted, whether or not it is a majority view. Knowing what our mult-faceted role is in today's global environment, we as citizens of the world should faithfully carry out our obligations so as not to aid in any crisis.

Our heroes

Our heroes are people who are a cut above the majority, the rest of us. They sacrifice their lives and relinquish daily comforts and stability in order that others can live in peace and comfort. They come in the form of firefighters, servicemen and servicewomen, train and bus operators, airline employees, sanitation workers and organizations, public and private utility companies and their staff, policemen and policewomen, postal service people, and millions of good-hearted and responsible volunteers across our communities providing unselfish public service in crises and also in peace. It is incumbent upon us to provide the necessary economic resources to enable these service people to continue to carry out their tasks.

Our leaders

Our past and present leaders deserve special mention here. They either work independently, in alliance with other like-minded individuals, or within government organizations to improve the lives of millions and direct people to contribute to worthy causes. Our leaders inspire others. They interact with and influence leaders of other states and countries to bring about peaceful settlements to international disputes and economic stability in the world. As part of businesses and institutions, leaders further the interests of the community in which they operate. Due to their unique role in the society, their success is measured by the good they create in the community.

Businesses

The underlying purpose in forming businesses and organizations is to pool together resources for attaining a business objective. Businesses range in size from a single person entity to a complex multinational organization. Globally there are currently millions of these types of institutions providing products and services either to their business associates or to the general public at large. People not only benefit from obtaining those services or products at affordable prices, but also invest in these corporations.

Like the human body, businesses need periodic checkups to make sure its vital functions are operating efficiently. This is done through both internal and external reporting of the financial affairs of a company, overseen by its officers, directors, outside accountants, corporate counsel, and regulators. Businesses need to comply with commerce laws and tax laws and contribute their fair share toward taxation.

In addition to attaining their financial purpose, businesses also get involved in their communities, by sponsoring events and providing internship opportunities. The actions or inactions of the businesses have far-reaching effects on other segments of society; therefore, they are expected to be sensitive to this fact and constantly monitor their activities to make sure they are in alliance with normal social order. In other words, businesses need to be cognizant of the corporate social responsibility they are expected to shoulder.

The three pillars of a civilized society are an individual and business progress evidenced by profits, social progress, and environmental sustainability. Therefore, it is important that this social element and an awareness of environmental sustainability are deeply embedded in our corporate culture.

Broadly speaking, the role of any business is to carry out its mission in a profitable manner to assure shareholder value, without jeopardizing the social good and sustainability. Organizations are expected to maintain and increase value for their stakeholders. It should be emphasized here that the shareholder value is merely a subset of the stakeholders, which encompass everyone affected by corporate actions. Corporations are expected to operate efficiently, legally, and within social bounds, and must also be transparent and accountable for all of their actions. Corporations are legal entities separate from their employees.

However, when management commits a violation or breach while carrying out their intended duties, that "corporate veil" or status is disregarded and the whole corporate structure is viewed under the microscope to bring the facts to the surface. As in the case of energy giant Enron, those powerful few at the top were corrupted by greed and violated the trust bestowed upon them. Sad but true, as George Orwell says in his *Animal Farm*, "power corrupts and absolute power corrupts absolutely." All of Enron went down, including Arthur Anderson, the outside accountants who failed in their due diligence and examination. Revealed through books and innumerable investigative articles in newspapers and magazines including an article in the May 2012 issue of *The CPA Journal*, the accounting irregularities disclosed by Enron in its reporting documents included the concealment of assets and liabilities (off of the balance sheet), the nondisclosure of related party transactions, corporate governance problems, and the over-statement of assets and equity. The transactions constructed based solely on accounting trickery lacked any substance. This reminds me of a humorous comment made by a partner in the accounting firm where I worked. Commenting on the carelessly slapped together financial statements, he said, "In the absence of substance, form is acceptable." Neither the people who prepare the statements nor the independent outside accountants seem to care about the substance any more.

The fall of Enron and numerous other corporate financial scandals brought about the 2002 enactment of the Public Company Accounting Reform and Investor Protection Act—popularly known as the Sarbanes-Oxley Act, or SOX. This act sets the code of conduct for those associated with corporate financial reporting, as well as the reporting by not-for-profit entities. This new compliance involves additional costs, which could have been avoided if those responsible for reporting had not been irresponsible. SOX also created the Public Company Accounting Oversight Board (PCAOB) to oversee the accounting profession. The new laws and regulations are intended to plug the loopholes in the old system and institute effective controls. They can only be fully effective if there is strict compliance and total regard for them. The SOX could not prevent the financial meltdown and sub-prime crisis. Similarly, an ongoing financial scandal dealing with London InterBank Offered Rate (LIBOR) could not be caught earlier. The facts about the financial irregularities are unfolding, and the ink on the recently enacted Dodd-Frank Act is still not dry. Are we to deduce from these episodes that we cannot simply allow the corporate world to be self-regulated and therefore must institute even stricter and broad measures, regulated from the outside?

There is also the ongoing discussion between government and the governance committees of major companies as to what is considered reasonable compensation for executives and what is excessive. Due to the complexity of the issue including various factors such as profitability, individual performance, industry practice, and economic condition, there may never be a clear guidance or a resolution on this issue. Unless objective criteria are found and agreed upon, this issue will continue to be a subjective concern of individual corporations.

United States President Calvin Coolidge once said "the business of America is business." The words were intended to uplift the entrepreneurial spirit of young America. It was not meant to cast a blind eye toward millions of disadvantaged people who are in need of timely help just to stay above water.

In a market economy within the democratic structure, our businesses are naturally empowered to reach any heights for themselves, and in the process create a social good by improving the lives of millions. Collective progress is only achieved if we channel all our energies toward that goal and become worthy of the mutual trust. Our business leaders need to assume their natural roles as community leaders to be held accountable for their actions. America would love to see business leaders and government officials on the same side of the aisle, working together toward common goals.

Professionals

Professionals, whether working independently

or with businesses or governments, have special skills through their advanced education and training (for example, accountants, doctors, lawyers, engineers, educators, and consultants). They have the most important role to play in these modern times. It is a unique role because not only do they have to abide by the code of conduct of their respective profession, but they have to display public trust at all times. The professional, moral, and social values are all interwoven in their makeup and they are made accountable for even the slightest departure from adherence to those values. Although they work very closely with businesses and other citizens, they must maintain a necessary distance from those they interact with, in order to remain objective and effective.

In performing their due diligence, professionals must adhere to the standards set forth by their professions, and above all meet the objective criteria expected of them by the general public. They must not hide behind their professional garb for protection. Their education, training, and experience must benefit the community. We should be grateful to young graduates who choose their respective professions, because they believe in the causes that matter. Such achievement comes after personal sacrifices, hard work, and abstaining from opportunities that are purely monetary in nature.

Governments

All governments, whether federal, state, and

local as well as foreign, have a huge impact on our lives, as citizens, individuals, businesses, organizations, and institutions. We are affected by tax policies, trade practices, economic policies and measures, and scores of issues both domestic and international. We are affected by world trade and conflicts, all the results of various governmental policies, actions, and the priorities set by them. Even after the people of the democratic form of government elected candidates and the party of their liking, they need to remain proactive and make sure the election promises are being honored by elected government officials. When an alternate course of action is taken that is a departure from an election pledge, there needs to be justification in doing so under the new set of circumstances. In times of peace, the evaluation and evolution of the government's role takes place continuously through media, public hearings, legislation, and peaceful demonstrations and rallies. During a period of conflict with outside countries, personal differences are usually set aside and there is a sense of solidarity supporting national interests. As we go about minding our own business, government makes laws, provides an oversight role, provides infrastructure, runs and funds various social programs, and provides domestic security and protection from border and international conflicts. The federal government carries out its duties and functions through departments and agencies, some under its direct control while others sponsored by it.

Through social media, interconnectivity is made easier today. It is possible for the public to become aware of government action and policies and understand better the role it is assuming. The same media has made it possible for the people to participate in the process through opinion polls and blogs. This has become increasingly important in election years as people are able to see the prevalent views, whether aligned with theirs or not. It is an important phenomenon by which a vast country such as ours can be brought close together in national dialogue on many key issues, including education, abortion, immigration, health care, foreign policies and trade, as well as issues specifically dealing with women and minorities. Hopefully, this can bring about the depolarization and unification of our country.

Looking at the dismal financial position of our country and that of its constituent businesses in general, we need strong economic and fiscal policies, including a major tax reform and financial regulations.

The 2013 tax law shifted the tax burden to higher earners and closed some of the tax loopholes. These are steps in the right direction toward bringing about fairness and equity in the tax system.

Government must continue to promote and subsidize businesses and sectors most likely and willing to create jobs here at home, without penalizing those who outsource in order to be more efficient and competitive. The issue of expatriating profits to evade taxes is a different matter, which should never be tolerated.

In the wake of the worst financial disaster, there is obviously a shift in the American Dream from owning a home to finding a decent job. There is a new trend of creating multifamily dwellings in place of the traditional single family homes. People should welcome this new sensible approach with open arms. It is encouraging to see average Americans coming up with creative ideas that do not rely too heavily on the government and the market forces that controlled and mortgaged their destinies not too long ago.

That leaves two other main areas of household finance, namely affordable education for adults and their children attending college, and an affordable mode of transportation. Governments, businesses, and educational institutions can certainly come up with cost cutting ideas and incentives to make education and transportation affordable for people to be able to sustain themselves in the foreseeable future. Without a coordinated effort by all the interested stakeholders, however, we are not going to get the job done. We live in a connected world. We simply cannot ignore and discount the way the rest of the world deals with domestic issues, approaches problems, and comes up with solutions for the wellbeing of their people. We ought to compare the household cost, the cost of education, transportation, and other basic necessities of all the countries vis-à-vis their trade practices and tax structure to arrive at workable models for our country. The progress of any country cannot be measured in terms of average growth and stray averages, which do not depict a true picture of the quality of life of all its citizens. Through this we need to address the income and wealth divide existing in this country and the rest of the industrialized world. While mainstream America tries to put its house in order, can we put those beauty contests, extravagant and lavish parties, and a survey of who made the cut on the Richest 400 this year on hold for a while? That is not too much to ask, is it?

Most of the partying is done under the government's watch but it cannot do much about it since they lack the proper resources to be fully informed. In order for them to be able to do their job properly, we need to provide efficient manpower and the right technology. As for the proper size of the government to be able to get the job done, the emphasis needs to be on "rightsizing" rather than "downsizing." Rightsizing implies the right number of people to run the program most efficiently. The same is true of the allocation of government funds for social programs. Initially a disproportionate amount needs to be injected for essential programs such as low income housing, free and subsidized education, and affordable health care, which in the long run pay for themselves as public health, high school scores, and depth of knowledge improve and we are once again able to compete academically with the rest of the world. Those contests we do need. We need to collaborate with the foreign governments, nongovernmental organizations, nonprofit organizations, and multilateral and international organizations who have the wealth of information and time tested solutions to the very problems that we are struggling to overcome. That can benefit us immensely in our efforts to rebuild our beautiful and great country.

Nongovernmental organizations

In addition to the national governments, people's lives are affected mostly positively by the efforts of other organizations, especially non-governmental organizations (NGOs). Wikipedia defines an NGO as a legally constituted organization created by natural or legal persons that operates independently from any form of government. NGOs can be local, national, or international in their scope and form. Although they may influence the governments or organizations to institute policies that favor their cause, they are neither political nor lobbying organizations. NGOs may work independently or with other organizations for humanitarian and other social causes to complement the work of governments and international and multilateral organizations. Due to their overreach in the communities they work, their mission and actions are closely watched, often with skepticism, especially when they are not aligned with the efforts of the local governments. In a global environment, the existence and work of NGOs and other international organizations that provide the necessary assistance, whether in dealing with a crisis due to a natural disaster or an epidemic, or in dealing with ongoing efforts toward development, play a very important role, working alongside the local government and other organizations. Therefore, we need to be open to, and be appreciative of, the efforts of these service providers. As pointed out in Wikipedia, NGOs derive their credibility through the 2002 establishment of their code of ethics by The World Association of Non-Governmental Organizations. These valuable organizations must be allowed to work independently to maximize their efforts in rebuilding the communities rather than work for the narrow interests of the corrupt local governments, which was seen in Haiti after the 2010 earthquake, may be corrupt.

Some examples of NGOs:

Amnesty International: deals with human rights issues and affords protection to those citizens of the world who otherwise would have felt vulnerable against international and national laws discriminating against them.

Oxfam: concerned with poverty alleviation, provides needy people with the equipment and skills to find food and clean water.

Afghanistan Information Management Services: provides specialized technical products and services to support development activities implemented on the ground by other organizations.

Nonprofit organizations and educational institutions

Nonprofit organizations (NPOs) and educational institutions are the drivers of our civilized human race. NPOs are formed to attain a mission or objective for a charitable, social, educational, or scientific purpose. Their funding is derived through general campaign, grants, government funding, the sale of promotional material, and special events. Most are formed under a tax-exempt status granted to them by the federal and local governments. The charter lists their organization's main purpose and mission. NPOs are run by professional staff and volunteers and are governed by an executive board. Educational institutions operate like NPOs with a team of administrators and an oversight board. In the aftermath of the financial crisis, many NPOs fell on hard times as individuals and businesses, who are their biggest contributors, also experienced tough times. For those entitled to government grants, the shortfall in government funding made matters worse. The educational institutions experienced less than normal returns on their endowment investments, resulting in shortfalls both for daily operating as well as expansion. Do not withdraw commitment to the causes you believe in, stand for, and are willing to make sacrifices for. This is exactly the time when our true character, our sense of beliefs, and our will to be charitable are tested. NPOs, a significant wheel in our economic machine, need all the respect and attention they badly deserve. Sadly enough, as I have observed and experienced in my casual conversations with people, many don't have the foggiest idea what these millions of NPOs do, nor do they understand their significance and role in our capitalistic setup. The perception of these NPOs and those associated with them leaves you with the impression they only deserve second class treatment. Yet it is encouraging to see many of our bright young graduates choose a career with an NPO over more lucrative Wall Street or corporate careers. I admire the courage and conviction of those proud parents and mentors who steer their wards in that direction and support their decisions.

Many NPOs have gained national and international stature for their dedication. There are a million others operating throughout the world, helping in their communities. It is the entrepreneurial spirit of our generation that has catalyzed the evolution of a plethora of organizations with social causes, even some with a hybrid profit motive blended with social causes. They can all coexist and flourish in perpetuity with the right nourishment and care, especially from the support of those who are fortunate to have built formidable fortunes for themselves. Examples of NPOs that have dedicated their efforts in broad ranging humanitarian issues include well-known organizations such as The United Way, Salvation Army, the Bill and Melinda Gates Foundation, Habitat for Humanity, Rotary International, Teach for America, The New Teacher Project (TNTP), Children's Christian Fund, Easter Seals, Red Cross, and the National Organization for Women (NOW). There are many regionally formed grassroots organizations that champion many worthy social and humanitarian causes in their community, including The Jewish Foundation for the Righteous, Young Audiences, Eden Autism, Enable Inc., and Workers Justice Center in New York.

In my career as an accountant and an auditor, I have worked with some of these organizations. It is impossible to measure the values these organizations and their staff create and nurture in monetary terms. They leave behind a legacy upon which our future success in sustainability will depend. Crisis or not, it is our social obligation to financially support these organizations so they can continue to carry out their mission and make a difference.

Multilateral organizations

Multilateral organizations or international organizations are formed to resolve by consensus and agreement the economic and political issues affecting either a single nation, groups of nations, or the world at large. The process is called multilateralism, which refers to multiple countries working in concert on a given issue. United Nations

(UN), World Bank Group, International Monetary Fund, and World Trade Organization (formerly General called the Agreement on Tariffs and Trade) are some of the major multilateral organizations. They were formed post-World War II around 1944 to 1948. These organizations have important roles to play in solving international conflicts, crises, and disputes. Most of the countries of the civilized world are constituent members of these organizations and are run by their governing bodies. In essence these organizations become "go-to entities" for problem resolution when the disputes or crises cannot be resolved internally by the affected countries or states. The enormous challenges these international organizations face in operating and succeeding in their goals cannot be overemphasized. Trying to achieve a consensus among members with diverse interests can be a monumental task. In addition, they can recognize the issues, planning, and execution to solve the crisis, dispute or a conflict, whether dealing with humanitarian issues, economic upheaval, or political uncertainty in a given region. As with any organization, these bodies are far from perfect. They may not have successfully solved every problem presented to them, but their role cannot be overlooked. In the ever increasing influence of global environment, a country cannot sustain itself without being affected by international forces. The multi-faceted roles of these international organizations become even more important.

The United Nations: The United Nations (UN) is an international organization founded in 1945 to maintain peace and security in the world, developing friendly relations among nations and promoting social and economic progress. One of its main purposes is to improve the lives of the poor while eliminating hunger, disease, and illiteracy. Currently the UN is working with The Earth Institute at Columbia University in New York, along with NGOs and other corporate partners, on Millennium Development Goals designed to significantly reduce hunger by 2015 and eliminate it totally by 2025. Other goals are to increase literacy especially among children, to resolve women's issues, and to achieve overall sustainability. Peace and order encompass dispute resolution, refugee protection, counter-terrorism, disarmament, nonproliferation, promote democracy, and establish and protect human rights. The UN functions through its principal organs, the General Assembly, the Security Council, the Economic and Social Council, the Secretariat, the International Court of Justice, and Trusteeship Council, which are further divided into organizations dealing with specific issues affecting member countries or the world at large. World Bank Group (WBG), International Monetary Fund (IMF), and World Trade Organization (WTO) are some of the key components of the UN system that help provide financial assistance, developing and creating and maintaining trade opportunities for the nations of the world.

World Bank Group: The World Bank Group (WBG) provides loans and grants at preferential rates and terms and other assistance to member countries for their development in education, health, agriculture, environmental protection, investment, and insurance and for providing infrastructure and assistance with governance issues.

International Monetary Fund: The International Monetary Fund (IMF) works to foster global growth and economic stability. It provides policy advice and financing to members in economic difficulties and works with developing nations to help them achieve macroeconomic stability and reduce poverty. The fund analyzes the appropriateness of each country's economic and financial policies for achieving orderly economic growth and assesses the consequences of those policies for other countries and for the global economy. Rather than requiring collateral from countries for loans, the IMF requires the government seeking assistance to correct its macroeconomic imbalances in the form of policy reform. If the conditions are not met, the funds are withheld. At times the IMF has been criticized for this requirement and blamed for exacerbating the crisis situation in some regions. Some reports suggest the IMF should have anticipated the crisis, or could have been more efficient in carrying out its policies and providing oversight function.

BRICS: BRICS is an acronym for an association of five major emerging economies:

Brazil, Russia, India, China, and South Africa. Originally it was named BRIC and its foreign ministers met in New York City in 2006 to begin high-level meetings. In 2010 South Africa joined them to form BRICS. As of 2014, the five BRICS countries represent almost 3 billion people, which is 40% of the world population. Since its inception, BRICS has held several meetings and summits to explore the means to improve the global economic situation and get involved in global affairs. In July 2014, BRICS agreed to create a $50 billion New Development Bank to fund infrastructure and other development projects in the BRICS countries. The group also announced the creation of the Contingent Reserve Arrangement (CRA), a $100 billion fund to provide short-term liquidity support to members of the group, similar to IMF. This will be funded by each of the members making a portion of their foreign exchange reserves available if any member was in need. The creation of this New Development Bank by BRICS may relieve the IMF of some of the burden it had to carry in the aftermath of the world financial crisis.

The World Trade Organization: The World Trade Organization (WTO) replaced the General Agreement on Tariffs and Trade (GATT). This organization deals with the regulation of trade between participating countries, providing a framework for negotiations and formalizing trade agreements and dispute resolution processes aimed at enforcing participants' adherence to WTO agreements, which are signed by representatives of member governments. Another priority of the WTO is to provide assistance for developing, least developed, and low income countries in transition to adjust to WTO rules and disciplines through technical cooperation and training. The WTO is a center of economic research and analysis; regular assessments of the global trade picture in its annual publication and research reports on specific topics are produced by this organization, which works closely with WBG and IMF.

These international organizations have been criticized from time to time for not accomplishing what they set out to do or not doing enough to deal with global issues. Their existence has rarely been questioned because the world would not be where it is today without the great efforts of these organizations and the extremely talented and dedicated people who run them. Thanks to the democratic and transparent environment in which these organizations operate, they have been able to make course corrections when needed in the ever changing global economic and political landscape. As always they need adequate support both in terms of fair contributions from member countries to operate efficiently and representation and voice to make important decisions in a timely manner. For their part these organizations must continue to educate people about the progress being made and communicate the problems the world could face in the foreseeable future because of the international implications of the actions by individual countries. While it is natural to put part of the blame on these organizations first for not measuring the pulse of the global economy in time to avoid the financial crisis and then for being generous with the bailout package to Greece, these are tough decisions that need to be made to repair the damage and stop the bleeding. Ultimately it is our responsibility as citizens of the world to participate in this democratic process by honestly exchanging ideas, information, expertise, and education that can benefit the entire world. Each country will deal with the aftermath in a way that will make the recovery possible with the least pain to its constituents; however, they should not shy away from their obligation to continue to promote world trade and abide by multilateral trade agreements. Only then we would be assured of long term growth.

Trade associations

Trade associations, whether formed as nonprofit organizations or not, further the interests of a group of companies or associations. They usually require membership fees for operation, which may include periodic meetings, networking events, publication of events, news and member directories, and education, benefitting their membership. Within their scope these associations may influence legislation that may have an effect on their membership. Their activities are under watch by governments, commerce, and businesses to make sure they are competitive. The role of these associations becomes even more important during crises because local businesses look to their leadership and peers for guidance, support, and resources to survive in uncertain business climate.

Lobbying groups

Lobbying is an act of influencing legislation. Its main purpose is to persuade legislators to either repeal, introduce, amend, or change a provision in the law or the entire act in the best interest of the group that the lobbying entity is representing. At its core is the exercise of the democratic right to be heard, especially if a particular legislation adversely affects a group that would otherwise have no recourse. The government or a legislative body is not sympathetic toward a lobbying activity that could jeopardize a larger public interest.

As we have seen, our lives are affected by diverse organizations and entities in some way just as events, both natural and man-made, alter our lives. Mostly it is what we do that determines our fate. Therefore, crisis or not, we ought to look at our shortcomings, mistakes, and liabilities, while at the same time cleaning our balance sheets because, if left alone, they could destroy everything we stand for, not just for us but for the rest of the world as well.

Chapter 3
The Role of Accountants

No person was ever honored for what he received. Honor has been the reward for what he gave.

Calvin Coolidge, 30th U. S. President

History and structure

The accounting profession in its present state has been around for over 100 years. As a matter of fact, the American Institute of Certified Public Accountants (AICPA), one of our oldest institutions in the United States celebrated its 125 anniversary in 2012. The early accounting can be traced to early civilizations such as Mesopotamia. By the time of the Emperor Augustus, the Roman government had access to detailed financial information (in the first century AD).

One's accounting career starts with obtaining 120 to 150 credit hours of intensive education in accounting, auditing, finance, taxation, management organization structure, and information systems, after which a graduate is encouraged to pass the Uniform Certified Public Accountancy (CPA) examination. This coveted designation opens the door for a new graduate, a passport to unlimited possibilities in public accounting in auditing, tax, and management information systems as well as corporate opportunities and jobs in education and government. Irrespective of the area of their expertise, the accountants must abide by the general code of ethics in order to serve the public and maintain their license.

In the light of the ever changing business environment and accounting scandals, it is important to understand the traditional role of an accountant and the issues surrounding that role.

Traditional role of an accountant

Traditionally, accountants were recognized for their role to provide the core services of reviewing and auditing the financial statements of their clients as well as provide tax services. As the nature of business and its practices evolved, so did accounting practices. It is important, therefore, to spell out clearly the respective roles for which accountants are hired and the nature and extent of their involvement. Perception becomes as important as the facts and must be duly weighed in while defining that role. Clearly, business needs expanded the accountants' role, which now includes serving as trusted advisors and consultants to the businesses. When these multifaceted services are provided by the same firm, it creates a conflict between the traditional role of accountants and that as business advisors. While this issue is being addressed by the profession internally, there is still an obvious disconnect with the public at large that fails to see the distinction between different sets of services and therefore expects the same high level of scrutiny from the accountants no matter what the nature of those services are.

Independence, objectivity, and professional skepticism

Independence, objectivity, and professional skepticism are traits that are at the core of how accountants operate and the perception it creates in the minds of all those who rely on their services, whether contracted for or not. It is not easy to do given the vastness of audience and all the potential stakeholders who may be affected, however minutely, by the financial data published. Accounting literature does exactly that. It prepares accountants for such unforeseen circumstances and requires them to display independence, objectivity, and professional skepticism at all times, in fact, as well as in appearance. Independence requires the accountant to disassociate himself from the client. Objectivity measures a performance against how a prudent person would have behaved or acted in a given set of facts. Again, the accounting and auditing standards promulgated by the accounting profession have done an excellent job of educating its members; however, when it comes to measuring it against the pulse of the public, there is a lack of agreement. Everyone needs to be on board on this issue by closing the expectation gap and to avoid costly lawsuits and waste of taxpayer money. Advocates of the accounting profession must do a better job of communicating well with the public and be transparent regarding their role and involvement during the reporting process. It is important for people to know there are different levels of services, each requiring different expertise and the extent of work. Accountants cannot be held responsible for areas beyond their scope, determined both subjectively as to the contractual agreement and objectively as commonly perceived by the public. It is understood by the stakeholders that accountants display healthy professional skepticism throughout the engagement in order to unearth any irregularities. Accountants have to prove they acted diligently if they are ever questioned in a court of law.

Concentration

There is a concern among the accounting profession and other outside business groups, such as the American Antitrust Institute, a tax-exempt organization, that there is a concentration of public company audits among big audit firms. The profession must address this issue, however uncomfortable it may be, to assure the public their interests are not compromised by a small number of large and influential firms controlling the audits of public companies. Due to the self-regulated nature of the accounting profession, its membership should chart its course in such a way that the public interest in not undermined.

Auditor rotation

In late 2012 the PCAOB requested public comments on the proposal to rotate auditors of public companies. This was initiated in the light of

PCAOB's findings of audit weaknesses during their annual reviews of public company audits. There was overwhelming opposition to such a proposal by both the accounting community as well as businesses. Costs and disruption in the reporting process were some of the main arguments. The Audit Integrity and Protection Act, which passed in the House on July 8, 2013, pending outcome in the Senate, banned mandatory audit firm rotation. PCAOB finally dropped the proposal. European Parliament, on the other hand, approved auditor rotation on April 3, 2014. European Internal Market and Services Commissioner Michel Barnier commented, "These new measures will reduce risks of excessive familiarity between statutory auditors and their clients, encourage fresh thinking, and limit conflicts of interest." The rules require European-listed companies, banks, and financial institutions to appoint a new auditor every 10 years, though this can be extended to 24 years if companies put their audit contract up for bid at the decade mark or appoint another audit firm to do a joint-audit. The conventional wisdom suggests in the long run the rotation would prove to be effective as it would render the public company audits more objective. In the United States, the independence issue could also be successfully resolved by instituting joint audits by different firms, rotation among them in a staggering fashion, and further by proper involvement of government and regulatory (SEC) representation during the audit process. This would also avoid costly and time-consuming follow-up, litigation, and regulatory impunity.

Tax reform

The accounting profession is working as partners with the United States Congress in overhauling our tax system that has become so complex, even tax experts find it difficult to comprehend. Every year new provisions are added, piling onto the already voluminous code several times larger than both testaments of the Bible combined. The profession must emphasize simplicity, fairness, equity, convenience in payments and reporting compliance, fair chance to plead cases on the grounds of reasonableness and economic feasibility when they present their case to the Congress rather than guarding the narrow interests of the business community they represent.

Standards overload

The profession must try and keep its overload of educational material, standards, regulations, and compliance in check for it to run efficiently both for its own sake as well as for the business community it serves. This goes for all the state societies in addition to the national institute, which sets the tone for others.

International standards

Since we operate in a global environment, it is important for our business and tax laws, accounting and auditing standards, and business practices to be in harmony with the universal order for comparability, healthy competition, and overall sustainability. America must retake its leadership role in this important area as well by gradually moving toward a much anticipated convergence.

Sustainability-oriented activities reporting

AICPA in its October 2013 paper, "Accounting for the Sustainability Cycle: How the Accounting Profession Can Add Value to Sustainability-Oriented Activities," emphasizes the importance of and need for accountants to get involved in the process of sustainable reporting and assurance services to give credibility to the published data on sustainability-oriented activities. A sustainable report gives information about economic, environmental, social, and governance performance of an organization. It is a fairly recent trend and has expanded over the last 20-plus years. These reports are guided by the Global Reporting Initiative (GRI), a nonprofit organization that produces one of the world's most prevalent standards for sustainability reporting. This enables all organizations to disclose results in a similar way to financial reporting. The accountants have an important role to play in the measurement of data in consultation with subject matter experts and in setting assurance standards, as the paper points out.

Operationally, the accounting profession needs

to rethink its priorities and disassociate itself from the quota system of rewarding professionals on the number of hours spent on each assignment, but rather reward them on the difference they make in real terms both for the firm as well as the society they serve. The overemphasis on size and competition takes us farther away from our role as public servants.

My profession, as well as the others, can regain the trust and faith of people by what we do and what we stand for. More importantly, we must educate and guide those in need about the environment in which they live and operate. It is our responsibility to be transparent about what we do and dispel the mystery behind "bean counting" We are not doing enough at the college level to impart the practical knowledge in the field of accounting and make graduates aware of the challenges when confronting the issues of ethics in the work place. There is a disconnect between what college graduates learn and how to apply that knowledge in the real world. More importantly, there is an expectation gap between what people perceive our role to be versus what we as accountants think it is. The financial disaster and numerous corporate financial scandals proved to be very costly for the corporations, general public, and the accounting profession. The outcome of these lawsuits will not decide the fate of our reporting practices because those decisions are only creating a patchwork of laws not likely to permanently repair the damage.

As new rules and laws are introduced, so will the schemes created to counter the controls that the new laws purport to achieve. This requires us to be even more vigilant and expand our role to insure accountability and transparency.

Chapter 4
Our Liabilities

Hate is like acid. It can damage the vessel in which it is stored as well as destroy the object on which it is poured.

Ann Landers, American Advice Columnist

During my long career as an accountant, I was occasionally showered with compliments that I was an asset to my organization. At the time it felt very good, and it usually motivated me to do even better. As time went by, to be good and valuable to my associates, the organization I worked for, and the business community I came in contact with became second nature to me. As time goes by, the universe of one's contacts expands exponentially and with that comes the difficult task of balancing those relationships. As pointed out earlier, the professional constantly confronts the issue of independence and conflict of interests and has to make hard, but right, choices to preserve both his individual and professional integrity. As an accountant, I learned in order to increase the net worth of an entity, its assets must appreciate in real terms and its liabilities be kept at a sustainable level for efficient operation. The same is true when evaluating the net worth of an individual. Our success as a civilized society is measured in the same manner by recognizing our assets, our liabilities, and burdens. Once we are able to identify clearly those assets and liabilities, a corrective action can be taken by focusing our energies in the right direction. These liabilities include wars, poverty, religious fanaticism, racism, classism, separatism, discrimination, misplaced priorities, inequalities, unethical behavior, and cheating.

Wars

We have fought among ourselves since time immemorial. The only difference is how we fight wars. Enormous amounts of time, effort, and money are spent in preparation and execution, also in prevention efforts and maintaining the balance of power in the world. In the ancient times, wars were fought between two enemies, principally on the field of action. Today they are fought more intellectually, intelligently, and strategically with the support of friendly countries and allied forces, because of the global impact they may have. In today's civilized world, wars serve no constructive purpose. They only accomplish the objectives of those few who instigate them. Throughout history there have been constant wars between groups with different ideological differences; the extreme example was the terrorist attack on U.S. civilians on 9/11/2001 in which thousands of innocent lives were lost. Hundreds of lives are lost every year in such senseless attacks worldwide. Wars cause human suffering during and after the conflict. Sometimes they last for years, causing economic havoc and social uncertainty in the region under attack. People around the world should rise as one to prohibit any kind of war and to remove it from the list of means to resolve an issue. National governments owe it to the world to do just that. National and international courts and tribunals should be responsible to try violators of human rights and justice. The powers of the UN or another universally accepted governing body must be expanded to deal with international crises and conflicts. A true representation is needed to assure impartial treatment. Only then will people trust one another, be able to trade with their global partners, and travel freely, expand their horizons, and spread goodwill. This is not an easy task, considering century-old traditions, changing balance of power before the Cold War and after, and the intelligence capital, and also because of our lack of knowledge about the cultures and lives of our neighbors as well as our intolerance toward the religious beliefs of others. The answer lies in educating ourselves adequately about the world and its people so it helps us overcome our shortcomings. For every liability that exists in our society, there is an asset available to offset its ill effects, if only we are wise enough to recognize them.

As hard as it is, we need to consciously make an effort to imagine a world without wars. Imagine the financial savings—enough to reach the Millennium Development Goal of eliminating world hunger sooner than anticipated. If only the nations and their leaders worked together for this worthy cause and gathered around a tree in Bodhi

Gaya, where the Buddha attained enlightenment and started sharing his wisdom about detachment and compassion with the peoples of the world. It would truly be a world changing event.

It is time to revisit our gun laws to ensure the safety of our children and of civilians. It is not possible to end wars and killings without changing ourselves and getting rid of many other poisons and damaging conditions we have created for ourselves as we traversed through time. Let us look at some of those.

Poverty

Poverty is the single most condition hindering our progress. It is a trap because poverty and dire economic conditions are usually the reasons for many conflicts (such as an external war, a civil war, or a coup intended to overthrow a government). These events leave the affected countries even poorer and their people sick with life threatening and chronic diseases.

Demographically our planet is divided into developed nations with advanced economic conditions, emerging or developing economies making marked progress over several decades, and underdeveloped regions. With approximately seven billion people, the bottom billion, or about a fifth of the world's population, lives in extreme poverty. These people are the subject of discussion in Paul Collier's book, *The Bottom Billion.* As Collier points out, the majority of these bottom billion live in Africa and Central Asia. According to him, poor people are mostly not able to dig themselves out of poverty because of the following four traps: the conflict trap, the natural resources trap, the trap of being landlocked with bad neighbors, and the trap of bad governance in a small country. These traps are not inescapable. Unfortunately there are external factors that do not make development easy. Collier cites some startling statistics contrasting the bottom billion with other developing countries:

	Bottom Billion	**Other Developing Countries**
Average Life Expectancy	50 years	75 years
Infant Mortality Rates (death prior to age 5)	14%	4%
Malnutrition in Children	36%	20%

These numbers are eye openers. If the poverty issue is left untreated and unattended, even more people will be thrust into that hole. Thanks to efforts being made in the past decade by the governments of the bottom billion people, and by the international community and multilateral agencies in dealing with the poverty, hopes have been revived somewhat with the commitment of the participating countries in setting the Millennium Development Goals, chief among them the eradication of extreme poverty and hunger by 2025. Through the Millennium Promise, the UN, the Earth

Institute at Columbia University, the business community, and international organizations have come together in partnership to institute, implement, and oversee the Millennium Village Project (MVP). In 2005-06 MVP was launched mainly in the poorest regions of Africa. Phase 1 showed encouraging results. The second phase will last through 2015. The MVP uses science-based interventions in five key sectors: business development, agriculture, health, education, and infrastructure (including water and sanitation). These projects place an emphasis on gender equality and environment sustainability. Once a year, the Millennium Promise encourages people to increase awareness around the globe and to "stand up and speak up" against poverty and hunger in their community. Participation can be increased through donations of money, materials, and services. There is still a long way to go to eradicate all poverty by 2025, as well as achieve other Millennium Development Goals dealing with improving education, infrastructure, women's issues, sustainability among the world's poorest people, and to remove inequality across the board.

Across the world business leaders and entrepreneurs have been successful when they create ways to deal with the issue of poverty. One innovator is Muhammad Yunus. He created micro-credit, and provided affordable opportunities to millions of Bangladeshi women to earn a modest living. Tired of only teaching economics in the classroom, he chose the "righteous path" and helped millions of poor in his country kindle their entrepreneurial spirit, and changed their lives forever. He shares that journey in his first book, *Banker to the Poor.* Building on this concept of shared prosperity, he built alliances with the world's multinational businesses to create and implement the idea of Social Business, explained fully in his second book, *Creating a World Without Poverty.* The motto of The Grameen Bank (or The Bank of the Poor) is to comprehend and implement common sense principles of borrowing, utilization of borrowed funds for the running of a small business, and repayment of loans on easy to manage small payments. No collateral or security is required. Loans are usually made to a group of borrowers who must exhibit discipline in order to not jeopardize other's chances due to their complacency. The bank associates work with the borrowers and periodically collect on the loans. The program goes beyond meeting the banking obligations of either party, as it also sets the principles and decisions to be followed by its members. The principles and decisions include discipline, unity, courage, and hard work in all walks of life, improving their lives and living conditions, eating healthy food, educating their children, creating and maintaining healthy sanitary conditions, not committing any injustice, helping one another, and staying physically fit. Thus Grameen Bank not only creates economic opportunities, but advances social reform at the grassroots level. In recognition of his work in dealing with poverty, Muhammad Yunus and members of his Grameen Bank were awarded the Nobel Peace Prize in 2006. In his acceptance speech in Norway and throughout his two books, Yunus emphasized poverty is a threat to peace and explained how it can be eliminated by empowering the poor through microcredit. The underlying faith comes from his belief, that of Gandhi and Mandela, and America's founding fathers, who stated all men are created equal. It is also important to realize those who have inherited poverty need that extra push and support to get started. His program, in addition to giving security free loans, also extends interest-free loans to street beggars and encourages them to sell small merchandise such as snacks, toys, and household items. The program has successfully pulled poor people out of extreme poverty and incorporated them into the mainstream of civilization. It will take decades of persistent efforts throughout the world in this area before any significant change can be observed.

Yunus, however, looks into a future in which poverty will only exist in the museums of the world. In the future, when school children tour the poverty museums, they will be horrified to see the misery and indignity that some human beings had to go through, he imagines. Many poor people, and low middle class people, today accept their condition as mere fate, not realizing what they inherited or what is thrust upon them is a result of a man-made disaster created out of inequality building up over eons. Would it not be wonderful to see the world without poverty in which the dreams of millions will become a reality?

The world economy is a lot more complex and comprehensive today than it was a century ago. Therefore, to push through this idea (which spread like wild fire in Bangladesh and other emerging economies) into other parts of the world, especially in developed nations, is not easy. This is because the traditional banking system has worked successfully—except when it has not. Yunus tried to introduce his small loan program in the United States and Europe. The concept was met with limited success, with some regions being more receptive than others in adopting the Grameen format or some other format close to it, while others failed. The program in Illinois has been successful, as well as ones in Poland, Norway, and Finland. Even such a modicum of success would not be possible in the developed world without the personal sacrifices of people such as Rosalind Copisarow, who resigned from her lucrative position at J. P. Morgan making loans greater than $100 million to take on a Grameen project in Poland making micro loans and change the lives of poor people in the bargain.

Part of the reason the unemployed and the poor in developed countries hesitate to borrow micro loans, or any loan for that matter, and start businesses is because under the current system they would lose their welfare benefits. The systems need to be there to protect those in need and facilitate the possibilities of self-employment and entrepreneurship. It needs to do away with outdated and rigid rules, bureaucracy, and unnecessary paper work that overwhelm laymen. Poverty will never be fully eliminated until we who are somewhat fortunate feel their pain and see the world through their prism.

There are a number of corporations that claim to display corporate social responsibility by mere volunteerism, which often serves as photo ops and a mention in their annual report about their involvement. I have seen those types walk away from a packed room gathered to hear Yunus at a book signing event, even before he started explaining about his microcredit and his vision of a poorless world. The poor of the world are without real representation, and their voices do not carry far enough. Poverty will not be eliminated as long as those who have plenty continue to scratch each other's back and refrain from sharing the resources and all the profits to be found in the present capitalistic setup. Grameen, through its micro loans, engages the poor, mainly women, to set up their own small shops or home grown businesses, on their way to self-sustenance. The social businesses in partnership with microcredit organizations take it one step further to benefit the local community and their well-being. The Grameen-Danone joint venture, for example, has created a brand of nutritious yogurt for the poor children of Bangladesh.

The social business is a no loss, non-dividend business. It is usually set up as an arm of a profit making entity. Capital is raised to set up a social business with a social purpose to achieve. The profit made from social business is ploughed back into the social business to further its mission. Unlike non-profits, which have to rely on ongoing support from private and public sources, the social business is a self-sustaining model financed by the investors and members.

In order to achieve social purpose, businesses can be inspired, for example, to set up cooperatives and credit unions under the corporate umbrella for the benefit of its needy employees where they can buy household goods and produce at affordable prices, borrow from the credit unions at affordable rates, and deposit savings for future needs such as education and housing. Employees can repay the loans through payroll deductions. By procuring from local producers and manufacturers directly, the extra layer of profit by middlemen can be eliminated and the savings will be passed onto the ultimate consumers, in this case, needy employees. Government can step in to provide subsidies, tax credits and relaxed capital requirements as an incentive to promote such social causes. The companies can take one step further in fully integrating employees at all levels, from thought process to decision making to implementation.

Every year hundreds of companies merge, close, or move operations for cost efficiencies, and, in the process, they jeopardize thousands of local jobs. The displaced workers neither have a say in the decision nor have appropriate representation. Consequently the local economy is severely damaged. Businesses must have a participative philosophy that instills a sense of belonging among employees, boosts morale, and gives them the sense they have made tangible contributions in building and helping the organizations to grow. Whenever possible, local entrepreneurs should be engaged as business partners to help the local economy to grow and sustain itself. The businesses can provide training and education to employees and their children who also can be considered for internship and future employment.

Yunus's Grameen family of companies promoting and practicing social business covers a wide array of sectors such as communication, technology, energy, manufacturing, food, and healthcare, which have shown proven success. It is hard to resign to the idea that such social business models could not work in a developed country, because millions of people are still below subsistence level and live in poor conditions. These people have no hope to escape from the poverty trap under the current capitalistic and free enterprise setup. They neither have the right clothing nor the deep pockets to get past the gate to a Fortune-land.

We have heard a million times from the immaculately dressed graduation and keynote speakers around the globe saying, "It takes a village," yet the concept hardly takes root in a tangible fashion. It gets forgotten even before the crowd disperses. We go back to our comfortable and socially and economically homogeneous lives. I miss Gandhi, that brown man in loin cloth who devoted his whole life toward fighting for the freedom of millions of poor people in India. He achieved more than that—he tried to bring about many social reforms in areas such as agriculture, education, women's issues, land reforms, and more. He denounced the century-old caste system and integrated the poor and untouchables into his *ashram,* giving them equal place in running his *ashram.* Although India has made some progress in these areas, it is far short of Gandhi's dreams. Half of the population still barely survives on less than $2 a day as income and wealth inequality between the rich and the poor continues to grow. Due to recent technological advancements, India's poor have easy access to mobile phones and other devices, but lag far behind in possessing other basic modern conveniences. Unfortunately, it is still dependent on the weather, particularly monsoons, for its agricultural output. The problem, though, is not insurmountable as modern techniques are implemented to trap and channel water for agriculture and hydroelectricity. It takes careful planning to utilize the limited resources for projects of such magnitude and assuring the success is not compromised by power play and corruption. In reality, India has been trapped for decades in this overdependence on weather for its agricultural needs and lack of effective governance due to corruption. In much of rural India, where the need for development and expansion is the most, very little progress has been made in providing the poor with adequate housing, sanitation, infrastructure, food, clothing, and education. Much remains unfulfilled of the election promises made, election after election. With each new election come new promises. It is encouraging to see the age-old act of defiance in the form of hunger strikes, propagated by Gandhi, still finds favor with the social activists in India and elsewhere. A recent hunger strike in 2013 by a prominent social activist in India was successful in compelling the government to deal with the corruption. That is a step in the right direction.

Every morning, rather than looking at the stock prices and house prices in the business section, we should look at unemployment data to see how many people were pulled out of poverty. We need to plan our day to ensure the common well-being. We should talk to our friends, neighbors, and even strangers to find out how they are really doing and how we can help to make any difference. We cannot always wait for the government and authorities to institute changes. Sometimes change has to come from within our small groups and communities by stepping up when we are needed. Democratic freedom grants us that choice to act on our own as long as our actions are not against public policy.

Religious fanaticism

Religions are as old as civilizations, and they will be with us for as long as we shall live. Simply put, they are nothing but beliefs inherited either through family lineage or our beliefs of choice.

There are some who are nonbelievers. By birth I am a Brahmin, a priest class in Hinduism, who is supposed to be knowledgeable in performing ceremonies and impart teachings of scriptures to common people. My upbringing, education, and exposure to people of diverse cultures and religions removed me far from the strict adherence to the religion of my roots. I believe in all religions or none at all. As I often argued with my grandfather while growing up, I firmly believed then, and I firmly believe now, no matter where we came from, what language we speak, and what religion we have inherited, we are all equal and it is our destiny to make the world a better place for all. If our religions, chosen or otherwise, have taught us anything of value and we become better because of it, then we should use that knowledge and power to unite us all and make this world a better place. No one religion is superior to the other. As we learn to respect all religions and therefore their people, we should always strive to find aspects common to all religions and become united, instead of separated by our differences.

I have no deep understanding or knowledge of the various religions. I do know this much: the overindulgence associated with religions and their underlying rituals have separated us from one another and have slowed human harmony and progress as is evident from the many conflicts around the world in the name of religious differences. We ought to look beyond our narrow beliefs and start embracing one another to focus our attention on the real problems of hunger, poverty, illiteracy, and pollution. There are abundant opportunities to cast those differences away and to imbibe the principles of humanity and spiritualism found in all religions. This can be achieved by proper education and creating among people of all faiths an awareness of common purpose and trust in one another, rather than doubting and resorting to false propaganda. We must value and respect all faiths for what they have to teach to all of whole humanity, without promoting the causes of individual religions whose success cannot be measured in terms of the wealth they have amassed and by the number of churches, temples, mosques, or synagogues built. Just as the world leaders get together periodically to assess the economic growth of the world, they should hold a world summit to assess the progress of humanity as influenced by their teachings and humanitarian deeds. Wouldn't that be wonderful? It is a mindless activity to gather numerical data on the number of people belonging to a particular religion or make geographical comparisons. Is that what our religions, our beliefs, and true conscience have taught us? Go to the streets to see how children mingle with each other and share those values, because they do not know any differences. We can learn from children.

As clichéd as it may sound, it is the children who are the future of our world. We owe them the assurance what they learn in schools will hold true when they grow up and take the reins from us. What good are those essay contests, if we don't follow the spirit behind them? "Dream loud," as one young adult repeats every time he pursues a social cause. Let us empower our youth to accomplish all they can for the betterment of our present and future and not hinder that progress by our actions influenced by rigid beliefs and prejudices. Every year beauty contestant finalists speak in favor of world peace. Ask any beauty queen. You will not find such unanimity anywhere else. We are so blinded if we ignored all signs. The clues are everywhere around us, like the "Coexist" bumper sticker with each letter signifying a different religion, but standing side by side. Whoever created it, thank you for sharing it with us.

Racism, classism, separatism and discrimination

Racism and classism, like religion, have separated our societies for as long as we can remember. Not as prevalent as before, and sometimes bordering on the benign, they still eat away at our true progress and must not be tolerated. When will we get rid of those stupid questions on applications asking for ethnicity and religion? What does that have to do with your qualities, achievements, and aspirations? How does it matter what you look like, or how tall you are, or where you come from? As hard as it is to believe in today's times, in this age of globalization, internationalization, and worldwide integration of diversity in almost all walks of life, racism, classism, and many forms of separatism and resulting discrimination continue to exist. We have all been victims of discrimination at some stage in our lives, whether or not we admit it. Even if we are discriminated in the name of these vices, we somehow tolerate such acts only so that we don't jeopardize our position, which could guarantee our ultimate success. There are times one must speak up or act against those forces and not compromise one's best judgment, which may call for personal sacrifices. Who is to say an accountant cannot express himself about issues other than accounting, think outside the box, and even look at critically the very profession that provided the education and training that helped him earn his livelihood? People must raise their voices and seek legal assistance if they are victims of class discrimination on mortgage applications, or passed for a job because of color, age, nationality, and sexual orientation, or even for their political views.

Newspapers and magazines are full of stories

that increase the awareness of the existence of these conditions and, more importantly, encourage those against whom such acts have been perpetrated to take proper action and ascertain their rights. The late Rosa Parks, an African-American who on December 1, 1955, refused to surrender her seat to a white passenger on a Montgomery, Alabama bus, triggered the boycott of city buses that practiced segregation. This and the series of civil rights actions that followed ultimately forced the courts to declare racial segregation unconstitutional. Many are today enjoying the freedom that would not have been possible without the courageous efforts of a few people endangering their lives. Thanks to organizations that provide the legal avenues to those for whom such services would otherwise be unaffordable. Government's role in supporting such causes needs to be complimented, especially in the wake of current financial difficulties.

Misplaced priorities

It is hard to be objective about setting priorities, especially as a group and more so while trying to bring a wider population on board. My own observations, influenced by my modest upbringing, have made me see things differently than others. Over time, some of those beliefs have grown stronger, even as I try to see other points of view. For example, I feel that we have our priorities misplaced. Professional sports and entertainment seem to be overrated, while education and teaching are underrated. Not that these are mutually exclusive and all activities are vital for survival and growth of individuals and societies but, especially when we are dealing with financial crises, there is a disproportionate share of national and personal wealth being diverted to the fields of sports, entertainment, glitter, fashion, and lavish parties, some as mere rituals while others as a vulgar display of wealth and power. The astronomical salaries and fees of celebrities and those in the entertainment industry did not go down during the aftermath of the crisis. These situations become even more glaring as we try to deal with real-world problems. Yes, the free world gives us choices. The wise will choose wisely so let us all join together on a journey of human decency to make social good for all, except this time we will make stops for everyone. Without them our journey will not be complete.

When seen through the eyes and minds of the Millennial, I feel more optimistic about our future. It is the responsibility of my generation to create a stable environment for them to work with. We need to reemphasize the value of sciences in education in order to enhance our technological progress and manufacturing capabilities, which will help increase the size of our economic pie for all to enjoy. Just to keep serving one another constantly is not going to increase real productivity but will only recirculate the resources among those who already have plenty. Education needs to be affordable, and educational institutions must bring down the cost of education by reallocating resources to research, cutting administrative costs, and bringing salaries down to sustainable levels. With mounting tuition debt and fewer job prospects upon graduation, the return on investment (ROI) in education doesn't look pretty. A nationwide revamping of our education system and underlying cost structure has to become our top priority.

Inequality

For many, inequality starts in the cradle and accompanies them to their grave. For others, it catches, either during formative years or their adult life, and they can't ever remove themselves from it. Some are fortunate enough to overcome its acute effects through their efforts and the choices they make throughout their lives. The unfortunate thing is the cumulative effect of inequality among our society has overshadowed any progress made. As outlined in *The Color of Wealth*, a book compiled by the nonprofit social group, United for a Fair Economy, in partnership with distinguished contributors in the field, a report called "State of the Dream: Enduring Disparities in Black and White," showed the level of racial economic disparity was largely unchanged between 1968 and 2001. The report further projects, for example, that at the current rate of improvement in black income compared to white income, it would take 581 years to reach income parity. One thing is certain: I will not be around to witness that historic moment. In short, it looks pretty dim. The same holds true even in emerging economies such as India and China. I recently visited India and witnessed the stark contrast between those who are rapidly moving up the wealth ladder and the millions still rotting in extreme poverty. The ever proliferating high rise towers with their gated status are next to slums with subhuman living conditions.

One of the drawbacks of a free market economy is that not all people have the same opportunities to be able to escape from poverty and hardship. Government, of course, can and does help to provide a necessary safety net and stimuli, but can only do so much. They are expected by the electorates and the representatives they elected to maintain a balance between being socially conscious and fiscally responsible. The change has to come from within our society, by the common people, through education and helping each other by promoting common interests and integrating all in the mainstream. This is possible only if those who have carved for themselves bigger shares of the economic pie either through inheritance, or as beneficiaries of generous benefits arising from business and social involvement, are willing to share that wealth with those unfortunate by sacrificing a little. It can be accomplished if this humungous task is broken up into an achievable set of goals, ultimately leading toward universal sustainability. Those simple tasks include getting involved in the community, volunteering, adopting programs and causes and working to assure their success, educating yourselves and others to create awareness of the problems, and seeking practical solutions in an unbiased manner. Such positive energy cannot be created without our willingness to channel the resources at our disposal (including time, money, services, and products) and a wealth of knowledge and information we are accumulating every day. On a social note, let your friends, neighbors, and colleagues know what you know and why and how you feel and get their feedback. Incorporate that feedback into the mix and utilize the collective wisdom and efforts to start the process of change. Track the progress and bring about the changes, even course corrections to stay true to its main objective.

George Packer writes about the state of inequality in our country in his essay, "The Broken Contract, Inequality and American Decline" in the December 2011 issue of "Foreign Affairs." He points out that "in the seventies corporate executives earned 40 times as much as their lowest paid employees. By 2007 the ratio was over 400 to 1. This widening gap and inequality has hardened the society into a class system, imprisoning people in the circumstances of their birth," as he rightly observes. He further reminds us "that inequality divides us from one another in schools, in neighborhoods, at work, on airplanes, in hospitals, in what we eat, in the condition of our bodies, in what we think, in our children's futures, in how we die." He goes on to say "inequality makes it harder to imagine the lives of others—which is one reason why the fate of over 14 million permanently unemployed Americans leaves so little impression in the county's political and media capitals."

Take the example of a middle class family trying to survive today in meeting its daily needs along with perhaps an occasional splurge of entertainment. From the price of a decent loaf of bread and milk to school supplies, clothing, transportation, a higher education down the road, cable and smartphones, to movie tickets and ever escalating prices at sports events and their concession stands, everything is getting further beyond the reach of many, all as a result of inequality in distribution of income and wealth.

Unethical behavior and cheating

Since the dawn of civilization, humans have lied, resorted to unethical behavior, and cheated aplenty, yours truly included. This is an undisputed fact. We are all guilty at some time or another, consciously or otherwise. There are scores of books written on ethics from law books to books of general interest and books of factual accounts of individual and corporate scandals. Even those who are supposed to impose laws and maintain law and order have been less than perfect as evidenced by revelations of corruption throughout the civilized world. Yet, we do not get it. Each time we read something or hear about another story involving cheating and unethical behavior, our resolve to rid ourselves of this evil gets stronger, but we become complacent and return to doing our things as usual. That is because cheating and unethical behavior is such an integral part of everyday life people do not even question it. Remember that famous line by President Richard Nixon during an interview by a British journalist David Frost, when he says, "But when the President does it, it is not illegal." If this behavior is left untreated and allowed to perpetuate itself, it will have serious consequences both to the perpetrator and those he comes in contact with in the community at large. David Clay Johnston in his book, *Perfectly Legal*, illustrates this point by recounting this story:

> *There is a fable of a village in wine country where each fall, after the grapes have been crushed and the vintage bottled, a bacchanal is held. Each vintner climbs a ladder in the town square and pours into a common cask a jug of his wine. One year the last vintner making the climb had fallen on hard times. The weather had not been kind to his grapes and he felt pinched. He decided that no one would notice if he thinned the wine with a jug of water. When he came down from the ladder, everyone applauded and the mayor swung a mallet to knock the cork from the base of the cask, out of which flowed clear water.*

Johnston aptly concludes the moral is that when one person cheats, no one but the cheat notices. But when everyone cheats, there is no party for anyone.

That is exactly what happened during our recent financial crisis. A vast number of businesses and individuals acted in self-interest, which ruined the financial and economic lives of millions of innocent bystanders. We are so preoccupied with quarterly results, revenue benchmarks, and stock prices that we have no time to measure our true value as promoters and protectors of social good in our society. Our schools and colleges do a good job of laying the foundation for moral and ethical behavior in their graduates; these qualities are left at the door when a graduate enters the business world and starts to climb the corporate ladder. This is the real world, he is told. Inexperience and innocence written all over their faces, they start their journey with dubious thoughts of what's right and what's wrong, a moral dilemma they may never resolve during their career. The courageous would venture to question the status quo and may even choose a righteous path, however treacherous its course. It is the task of all of us who have been around long enough and who are witness to many disasters to steer our youth in the right direction and provide the guidance and the encouragement necessary for them to succeed in the midst of uncertainty and disarray. We must impart that wisdom by setting examples and making personal sacrifices.

The answer does not lie in just working from

the outside and policing the systems so we can punish as many people as possible. The idea is to educate people to do the right thing and reward them for ethical behavior. Our schools, homes, social service firms and workplaces should work in lockstep toward a common goal to create an environment conducive to ethical behavior. For that we need to have controls in place, both self-imposed and external to keep us all on course.

It is not that these controls are nonexistent and that there is outright disregard for good behavior. It is that we have not been able to practice them and respect them at a sustainable level. Due to our inability and unwillingness to hold ourselves accountable for every action, we face unpleasant consequences. Our reactive instincts force us to put together a patchwork of statutes that do not necessarily provide the guarantee against future crises. If SOX could cure all corporate evil, we would not have had the recent crisis. It is the collective efforts of all responsible for smooth operation of corporate dealings that ensure a steady course. Every day people are forced to compromise their ideals and principles to commit acts that they are not too proud of. In the name of practicality and business sense, they pass as survivors. People these days no longer know their job descriptions. They are identified with their affiliations and interest groups working solely for their benefit, no matter what social damage it may cause in the process. People are asked to be quiet and side with their superiors when they know their superiors are in the wrong. Their job, raise, promotion, other tangible benefits, and a good reference for future opportunities are all at stake. Such is the awesome power of the necessity to survive. Against this huge force individuals feel powerless and vulnerable. At a personal level we are presented with the opportunities to work the system to our advantage and enjoy the small benefit of reduced premium upgrades, and extension in services, and a bank or an invoice error in our favor and many freebees that we somehow feel compelled to have. Sometimes this requires small lies and distortions of facts and data which we become so good at and after even feel comfortable with. We lie about our age, our height, our income, dependents, our deductions and expenses on tax returns, and it doesn't stop there. Most of us do not even realize there is a price to pay, and usually it is someone else who pays it. It may be in the form of increased premium, downgrade in services, termination of services, and costs someone has to pay because you cheated.

Picture this: A championship or a Grand Slam title may literally be on the line. Would you cheat? Only you can answer that question.

The reason why most of the people don't like to pay taxes is because they fail to see the social and economic benefits that result from the revenue collected by the government. U.S. Supreme Court Justice Oliver Wendell Homes Jr. once said, "Taxes are what we pay for civilized society." Many taxpayers fail to see this. Even the government is partly blamed for not educating the people enough so that they see the correlation between paying the taxes and the tangible benefits they derive from it either individually or as a group. There are enough tax expenditures enacted in the current income tax law benefitting taxpayers, such as home mortgage deduction, social security, retirement benefits, charitable contribution deductions, personal exemptions, earned income credit for low income individuals, etc., which reduce the effective rates at which they pay taxes. Non-filing of taxes, taking unsubstantiated deductions, non-reporting of income, and claiming unqualified tax credits all cost government billions of dollars in lost revenues each year.

David Callahan in his book, *The Cheating Culture, Why Americans Are DOING WRONG To Get Ahead*, narrates stories of people of all sizes, shapes, and stature who are very much part of the culture breeding in what he prefers to call Temptation Nation. Presented with an opportunity, almost everyone cheats, as was evidenced by Callahan in the following example. When the Twin Towers came down in downtown Manhattan on 9/11, the computer link between the New York Cash Exchange (NYCE) and ATMs at Municipal Credit Union of New York City was severed. As a result NYCE could not track ATM transactions and could not prevent members from overdrawing their accounts. People used ATM machines as cash cows and made countless withdrawals en masse. When the system was finally restored, letters were sent out to those with overdrawn accounts and those not complying were dealt with resulting in scores of arrests.

We live in a society with an "everybody does it so it must be okay" mentality. We are rigging the very systems that are trying to make our lives comfortable and our environment sustainable. Our tendency to constantly desire short term success and pleasure without worrying about the long term consequences will gamble away our future.

What motivates this unethical behavior? It could be as simple as trying to get out of a tough spot, to a more serious condition of behavior resulting in assumption of economic gain or power in an unfair manner. Inequality, hard times, discrimination and abuse, peer pressure, and other unpleasant circumstances may force even those with otherwise moral tendencies to deviate in that moment for a short term reprieve. This muddies up the water forever, which is only good for those who feel comfortable operating in such a polluted environment.

Every day there are stories about human tragedies and human rights violations committed by businesses, often ignored by officials and overseers. Hundreds of garment workers lost their lives in April 2013 in a collapse of a factory building in Bangladesh, as a result of inaction by the owners and authorities, even when the poor structure and cracks in walls were brought to their attention. Earlier, many lost their lives in a fire in the same industrial complex because once again fire code violations were ignored. Local and international communities raised their concerns in no uncertain terms, which should (hopefully) force the local businesses, the authorities, and their foreign business partners for whom the garments were manufactured, to take appropriate action.

The issue is more involved than just dealing with working conditions and the safety of workers, which obviously is of prime concern. It entails a compounding effect of many contributing factors such as business policies and practices both domestic and international, globalization, government trade policies, tax policies, and the extent and effectiveness of multilateral organizations. Fair practices and cooperation and full knowledge and understanding by all the stakeholders are as important as the rules and their compliance. It must be emphasized again that inequality is not just a domestic issue within the boundaries of each state; it is an international issue especially in a global business environment in which we are operating. To clarify that point, the objective of globalization cannot be just to achieve narrow business and individual gains but also to improve the working conditions of those workers, who for a miserly daily wage risk and compromise their lives. Compensation for those at the helm of multinational corporations have gone up astronomically, while that of the workers remained stagnant at between $1 and $3 a day, without regard to inflation.

The question is how must one deal with these issues? In order to be socially conscious and to show our support for humanitarian endeavors, should we buy these products made in foreign countries so the needy can continue to make a living or boycott those products to stand up against inhumane practices over the world? It is debatable.

We have enough problems on our hands that need to be dealt with in a hurry before they get out of hand. It will require both individual and collective efforts in a coordinated fashion to free ourselves from the burdens of our liabilities and increase our assets so our net worth will go up. It will have to be done ethically and responsibly so our reported assets represent their true values, a strong foundation upon which our future can be built and sustained. We need to establish "code of conduct" whether at home, at school, or at work and integrate that in our daily lives. We must create an ideal environment for it and not tolerate any infractions. Accountability and transparency must become essential ingredients for it to work. With common sense and a basic knowledge in house finance, for example, each unit can chart its course and monitor it so that adjustments can be made if plans change. It is also important for individuals to be aware of the economic environment, which may have a direct impact on their personal finances. It may be necessary to pay that visit to your advisor from time to time and help him help you stay on course.

Every year around the holidays, my wife and I try to watch that timeless classic *Fiddler on the Roof* starring Topol. Simple, meaningful lives of Russian Jews during the czar rule are portrayed beautifully in this movie. Who can forget that memorable line in a lyric, “If I were a rich man,” which speaks for all of humanity. It got me thinking, if I had a billion dollars to spare it would be enough to instantly remove 25,000 from acute poverty, without debate about social reform and other fancy terms. Tell me if I am wrong: My guess is, and this is an accountant’s guess, right now, right at this moment, there is enough wealth in this world ready to be redistributed, to take those billion or so instantly out of acute poverty and on their way to recovery and a bright future. This can be done, holiday spirit or not, without further ado and without those unproductive talks at the economic summits. Find them in shelters where there is no heat or air conditioning, where women are afraid of attack in their communal bathrooms with no security, under the bridges, in the subway tunnels, in the hutments, and every nook and cranny where they are hiding their poverty and shame. You will not need your MapQuests and GPS to find them. Just look around you. They are everywhere.

Part II:

Recipe for Survival

CHAPTER 5
Our Assets

Character and personal force are the only investments that are worth anything.

Walt Whitman, American Poet

Auditing companies and reviewing their books taught me a lot about their reported assets. In order to recognize and appreciate the assets and values in our society and in the world around us, though, you must have the sense of social responsibility deeply embedded in your DNA. It is our social obligation to preserve the social assets around us and even create more as we go along.

Albert Einstein once said, "Intellectuals solve problems, geniuses prevent them." Financial guru Warren Buffett, one of the shrewdest investors of our time, succeeded by drawing parallels between his work and the outside world to explain the philosophy behind his decisions. Even in his 80s, he has the smile and inquisitiveness of an eight-year-old. He is one of those few wealthy souls who want to share their wealth with others and is leading a group of socially conscious citizens who want to bear a greater tax burden, to the extent that a new tax code dealing with taxing the rich is called the "Buffet rule," after him.

Simply put, assets are what we own individually or collectively as organizations. Companies report assets on their balance sheets, along with their liabilities or obligations. Their net worth or strength at a given point is determined by the net assets left after fulfilling its liabilities or obligations.

Similarly in our social setup, our social net worth is what is left after satisfying our social obligations or liabilities. We have a moral obligation to increase our net worth by reducing our liabilities (see Chapter 4) and meeting our social goals. As human beings, we are also considered assets in the form of human capital. We are the most important component of social assets and are a driving force that makes the creation and sustenance of social net worth at all possible. We create both physical as well as social assets, and our success as humankind is also judged by the economic and social good we generate.

So what are these social assets? They include our good deeds as responsible citizens, such as fighting hunger, maintaining peace, improving and enhancing education, knowledge, fighting inequality, discrimination and human rights violations, helping one another without boundaries, understanding one another without prejudice, and finding common ground where differences occur, learning to coexist. Nelson Mandela once said about education in the social context, “If you talk to a man in a language he understands that goes to his head. If you talk to him in his language that goes to his heart.” The idea is to facilitate communication between people irrespective of their castes, creeds, nationalities, sex, age, and their affiliations because it helps serve a common economic and social purpose.

As the history of the world is updated, both our good deeds and our misdeeds are scripted side by side. Those who are wise will learn from them, but more importantly they will help create their own legacy. That is only possible if we appreciate, understand, and protect the social assets and our natural resources.

Human values

What are our human values? They include being honest, helpful, faithful, courageous, respectful, loving, responsible, humble, have a sense of sacrifice, a sound judgment, and seeking truth and fairness. In some measure we are all born with some or even all of these qualities, but we only fully and truly recognize and appreciate them through our life's journey. Through education, practice, and our upbringing we are taught about them. We are inspired by great historical leaders, such as Mahatma Gandhi. Gandhi spent his lifetime practicing and perfecting his human values through his quest to free India and the millions of people destitute under British imperialism, his fearless fight against the discrimination of colored people in South Africa and fighting in his country, and his fight against age-old customs and barriers to improve the lot of women, children, and those of lower castes. Someday we may be fortunate to create our own legacy, but we should always be equal to the task of fulfilling legacies we have inherited. We must keep the torch burning. Gandhi, respected as "Mahatma," or great soul by his followers and millions around the world, constantly drew his inspiration from Socrates, Ruskin, Tolstoy, and others and imbibed the salient features of Hinduism, Christianity, Islam, Buddhism, Jainism, and other religions to guide him. However, he never felt the need to visit places of worship. He found God in the hearts and smiles of children, poor souls, in human deeds, and through seeking Truth. He titled his autobiography, *The Story of My Experiments with Truth.*

Unfortunately, there are still parts of the world ruled by authoritarian and totalitarian governments. This has hindered our progress and shaken the confidence of people around the globe. Most people and governments still believe in world peace and harmony. We must find a peaceful and diplomatic way to convince the few who think otherwise. We need to educate everyone about the dangers of conflicts and the bleak prospect of human extinction if nothing is done about it.

In 1945, World War II ended and the United Nations (UN) was formed. The purpose of the UN was to bring harmony and peace among the nations by resolving disputes and conflicts peacefully around the table, instead of on a battlefield. Over the years, its role has expanded to deal with development before and after conflicts through diplomatic and strategic means. Through its multifaceted arms and affiliates, the UN has assumed a broader role of improving human conditions. No one disputes progress has been made, but this progress has been uneven because billions of people are still making less than $2 a day in a world economy that has expanded many fold since 1945. Once we are able to deal with the inequalities in our systems, it will be much easier to bring those bottom billion out of the hole. As governments, multinational and humanitarian organizations around the globe continue in this fight, so must the efforts of social activists at the grassroots level in our local communities. There are many, such as my uncle in India, who roll up their sleeves each day and run to where help is needed. My uncle calls himself a "non-professional beggar," because he approaches the well-to-do to spare what they can, in order for him to supply the needs of the destitute. He jumps on a train with bags full of goodies to be distributed to distant villages. He is helping to remove poverty through one random act of kindness at a time.

Ideas and vision

Ideas become assets when they create and add value for individuals, organizations, or society at large. In order to retain our values, we need to be in search of new ideas from a variety of places. In the last century, we saw and benefitted from revolutionary ideas of nonviolence and noncooperation conceived by Gandhi and practiced globally to deal with violation of human rights. The non-violence, non-cooperation tool evolved from Gandhi's principles of Satyagraha, which simply means "*Insistence* on the Truth." He first experimented with the idea of Satyagraha as a young lawyer and a social activist in South Africa fighting against unjust tax laws imposed on Indians living there. He practiced it again in India fighting against civil laws and later during his struggle for Independence from British rule. The act of Satyagraha and nonviolent civil disobedience was staged to provoke the enemy who would otherwise not react. A word of caution as pointed out by Gandhi on the practice of Satyagraha: "A Satyagrahi (meaning the person practicing Satyagraha) obeys the laws of society intelligently and of his own free will, because he considers it to be his sacred duty to do so. It is only when a person has thus obeyed the laws of society scrupulously that he is in a position to judge as to which particular rules are good and just and which are unjust and iniquitous. Only then does the right accrue to him of the civil disobedience of certain laws in well-defined circumstances." This is not some random or ad hoc disobedience of laws at will without regard to public policy. Social activists over the world practice Satyagraha by protesting and even fasting to air their concerns regarding human rights. Dr. Martin Luther King's march on Washington and his famous "I have a dream" speech are examples of the nonviolence and noncooperation movement. The fight against discrimination must go on as it has not been fully eradicated.

Eighteenth century explorer James Holman, though clinically blind at an early age, had a vision most of us do not have. Holman, a British marine, could not see if someone was colored or not, or if someone was tall, short, beautiful, or otherwise. Yet he could distinguish between right and wrong. His handicap did not prevent him from exploring the world, circumnavigating the globe five times and writing about his experiences without being self-promotional. Among his many causes, he fought the slave trade in Africa (where the Holman River was named in his honor). Being clinically blind, he could not physically see the beautiful landscape he was so close to, yet his sense of the world was quite accurate. This was mirrored in his mind as "soundscape," when he gauged the vastness of his surrounding by the sound of whispering winds. Holman's life and his faded footsteps are captured in Jason Roberts' fascinating book, *A Sense of the World.* Nature was very much alive for Holman. He probably captured more through his senses and imagination than we would, due to our biases and narrow visions.

Education

If raw and impure rocks can be cultivated into beautiful diamonds, so can we reshape and add a sparkle to our lives so that the glow will benefit mankind. But what is our guiding source for all this to happen? That would be education.

Many good deeds have started on instinct, by a fire within, or simply by being alert and aware of our surroundings. For good programs to sustain in a complex world environment, however, we need solid, ongoing education and training. With the advent of the Internet, the spread of knowledge and education opportunities have multiplied. Web-based knowledge has levelled the field for all who seek information. Online education has become a cheap alternative for those who find traditional education unaffordable. It cannot replace institutions through which the world's greatest leaders have passed. Lately, due to the astronomical costs involved, higher education seems to have unfortunately become a privilege only few can afford. Those who know it is beyond their reach make a tough choice of attending premier yet pricy institutions and incur an unmanageable amount of debt in the process, or. The price of inequality in our society today has outpaced inflation by many fold. President Barack Obama's thoughts became a testimony to this pressing issue when he recently commented, "I am absolutely committed to making sure that here in America, nobody is denied a college education, nobody is denied a chance to pursue their dreams, nobody is denied a chance to make the most in life just because they can't afford it. We are a better country than that, and we need to act like it."

In the next few years it will become clear whether those in power in the United States come to this realization and do everything they can to deliver on their commitment. If we were to claim the rest of the world looks up to us, we must prove that it works here at home before we can confidently prescribe these solutions to others. It requires a joint effort of everyone in a position to exert the influence to repair our education system and make higher education affordable. In this regard President Obama openly challenged university administrators to get a handle on rising costs. There is a proposal to forego some of the federal loans and to change the administration of college loan funds to make it more efficient. Other fiscal measures on the table include tripling the college tax credit for middle income families, more support for Pell grants, and changes meant to help students repay college loans more easily.

As our nation's leading institutions are done cleaning the mess from their last graduation celebrations, the time has come to make room for the new aspiring students. This time around they need answers and concrete promises before they mortgage their precious years away. It remains to be seen who leads the pack in freezing the cost of education or even boldly slashing it so that young dreams may have any chance of being realized. Some, such as the late Ray Bradbury, author of *Fahrenheit 451*, will somehow find a way to achieve education against all odds. Deprived of a college education because he could not afford it, Bradbury educated himself by spending countless hours at libraries (still free and the greatest living institutions of knowledge in our country). As was noted in his 2012 obituary in the *Wall Street Journal*, Bradbury wrote his famous novel on a rented typewriter in the library basement of the University of California, Los Angeles. Being from an older school of thought, he was skeptical of technology, the Internet and cell phones and resisted the conversion of his titles as e-books.

Not many of us have that kind of resolve and discipline to achieve what we set out to do. Most of us need constant guidance, care, direction, and above all means to achieve even our basic goals. It is not too much to expect society to contribute fairly. The individual achievements of our heroes will always to guide and inspire us, but our success as a society will only rest on our collective wisdom, efforts, and our commitment to coexist.

Social programs

In *Man and Superman,* Irish dramatist and socialist George Bernard Shaw described social entrepreneurs as unreasonable people and had this to say about them: "The reasonable man adapts himself to the world. The unreasonable one persists in trying to adapt the world to adapt to himself. All progress, therefore, depends on the unreasonable man." That mostly is true of all social activists and entrepreneurs. They have a mission to accomplish with a higher calling than their self-interests. Social entrepreneurs are self- motivated. Their lives are not rule-based but principle-based. They do not need titles as a measure of their personal success. These free-spirited individuals, through their organizations, have continued to contribute social value throughout history. They are a breed apart. They are the catalysts who facilitate action but as their roles constantly evolve, they also interact as principals to advance their causes. They are not afraid to break barriers and norms to achieve their goals to preserve human integrity. These individuals operate either with or without a political agenda as NGOs, or as nonprofit entities formed to advance a particular scientific, religious, educational, or humanitarian purpose.

Social programs, and social activists who run them, are our social assets because they add value to our social lives and protect them. They are our heroes and deserve our respect and recognition. In tough economic times they need help from us to carry out their missions. Many will fail due to lack of funds, lack of recognition, lack of community support, and lack of encouragement. That is a shame. I, for one, do not want those who chose these noble careers to become disheartened and lose faith in their beliefs. I beg them not to second guess themselves and be overly concerned about their economic future. One must be inspired by people such as Gandhi, Dr. King, Mother Theresa, Florence Nightingale, and so many others who sacrificed so much to improve the lives of millions. To paraphrase President Abraham Lincoln, you may not get recognized for what you do, but your actions should always be worthy of recognition.

Corporate social responsibility

Corporate social responsibility (CSR) is about companies and institutions being aware of their social surroundings and the positive impact their actions generate, which benefits society at large. As businesses become more integrated, global, and transparent, the awareness of CSR being an integral part of any business dealing is increased and can be measured in objective terms, which can be compared with similar businesses. As pointed out in Chapter 3, the world's major organizations are already reporting under the Global Reporting Initiative on their sustainability-oriented activities.

In the end, it boils down to being educated, aware, responsible, and above all accountable for your actions. No matter the degree to which each organization is aware of this broader responsibility and acts accordingly, they will all have to conform to some objective criteria or standards. Unless CSR is integrated into the corporate mission, its use will only be ad hoc and will only serve as self-promotion. Corporations need to be proactively seeking CSR in their hiring process, with current staff and all levels of managers, and in interactions with their suppliers and customers. Corporations need to refuse to deal with suppliers and customers who seriously lack CSR.

Profitability vs. sustainability

It is inherent in human nature to seek profits and benefit from one's efforts. The positive results from human efforts need to be complimented and rewarded as long as they accrue social benefit. In an ideal situation in which everyone is aware of one's responsibility to create social and economic good through their efforts, profitability and sustainability are mutually inclusive. That harmony becomes compromised once individual profits and interests take priority over the larger social and economic good. In the long run, pollution, loss of jobs in the community, loss of opportunities, cut-throat competition, and depletion of natural resources make economies unsustainable. All stakeholders need to be educated, informed, and vigilant at all times to try to stop and reverse these decaying conditions. In the modern world these problems are not just local; they invariably have global consequences. Often these conditions that inhibit our growth are both the cause and consequence of bad political decisions and power play. Take, for example, our crumbling infrastructure at home. Robert Frank (economics professor at the Johnson Graduate School of Management at Cornell University) shared his concerns in this regard in *The New York Times* in September 12, 2010 issue under the topic, "Building the Bridges to a Sustainable Recovery." He agreed with President Obama's proposal to create a $50 billion infrastructure renewal bank. That would partly solve the problem of this underfunded sector of our huge economy. This measure is still pending approval by the Congress. The data also list the United States as having one of the lowest percentages, about 2.5% of the gross domestic product spent on infrastructure among industrial nations. According to data compiled by the Civil Engineers Society, in the next five years, planned spending for infrastructure such as roads, water, energy, and schools among others will fall short of needed investment by a cumulative total of $1.8 trillion.

The government is not currently overspending on social programs; it's the other way around. Balancing the budget is a long term objective that could only be achieved if we pump enough stimulus into the economy to reenergize itself by increasing jobs, creating and maintaining safe and modern infrastructure and distribution channels, and providing quality affordable education. The revenue needs to be raised by increasing the individual taxes for high earner taxpayers and reforming corporate taxes so corporations pay on their true profits, irrespective of where they earned these profits. We need to invoke an ethical culture in our systems in order to understand our responsibility and recognize we are all on the same side. We need reforms and oversights because, based on continued financial scandals (both in the private sector and at governmental agencies), it is evident we are not ready for self-regulation.

There will always be strong resistance to new laws, regulations, and reforms as they seek to change the status quo and deal with the self-interests of those in charge. Take, for example, the recommendation by the PCAOB to institute the mandatory rotation of auditors of public companies every few years. The objective is to make these public company audits more effective and reliable and promote auditor independence. As reported recently by Reuters, the U. S. House Financial Services Committee unanimously approved a bill to prohibit mandatory rotation of auditors. This is not just about management decisions and short term costs involved with the rotation every few years. This is about the interests of all the stakeholders who rely on the financial statements of publicly held companies and are affected by their actions. They can only be assured if the financial statements are blessed by a group of highly independent professionals who represent a wider public and will therefore protect public interest. The answer may lie in formulating a team of independent auditors from more than one accounting firm termed "Joint Auditors," subject to rotation, for example, every 5 to 10 years, with appropriate representation from regulatory bodies and the oversight board at the inception of and during the audit process of each audit, rather than after the fact as it is done now. The presence of oversight and controls at all times would prevent fraud and financial misconduct. Paul Volcker, the former Chairmen of the Federal

Reserve Board from August 1979 to August 1987, is among the notables who favor requiring audit firm rotation and believes it would keep the firms from becoming too cozy with corporate management.

As a step further, as noted under CSR, the auditors someday will also be responsible to give assurance on the corporation's sustainability efforts. No doubt they will also evaluate the ethical leadership or lack thereof among businesses. Such benchmarks and definitions are already being integrated in corporate literature and culture, as recently pointed out by *ASA*–South Africa's leading accountancy journal. It contends ethical leaders always take the right path, even if the consequences are not necessarily palatable to a certain category of stakeholders. Ultimately, the leader will be recognized and rewarded, though not always financially, for taking the right path.

Using sustainability as our goal, our sense of ethics, and our sense of the world, will enable us to protect animals and other wildlife and also maintain and respect the ecological balance and natural phenomena. How can the killing of innocent animals be considered a hobby or a sport? The debate and fight between those believing in animal rights versus those who are opposed to it will continue with no end in sight. For the sake of sustainability of our planet, we need to keep fighting to protect the animals.

All around us are lessons on ethics, sustainability, and being a plain old Good

Samaritan. I am reminded of a life lesson I once heard from a sage when he blessed my cousin Sanjiv on his 50th birthday. He narrated a story of a new man in town trying to figure out if it was a good idea to move into a town that he was passing by. While passing through a cemetery, he observed that practically every tomb listed the age of the deceased to be in single digits, some aged two, some five, but no one over nine years old. This obviously concerned him, and he immediately turned for explanation to a wise man tending to the affairs of the cemetery and ceremonies. He asked, "Why did all these people die so young?" The wise man answered, "We here in this town only list the age of the deceased in terms of the numbers of years he or she spent helping others and creating social good." We all have to figure out what we need to do to improve our score of good deeds and the net increase in our giving, over our taking.

I look at my wife and my children and am proud to say I see, in their dealings with the world, a generous quotient of giving. Personally I do not have to go too far to look for role models. Lottery winnings and lucky breaks will only help people increase their physical assets but not increase their social net worth. The sooner everyone understands this, the better it will be.

Recipe for survival

Ultimately, most of us will survive the most recent economic disaster; however, some will pay a heavier price than others. Rather than simply finding solutions to help us repair and improve our economic lives, we must address this issue globally so everyone survives. We need to draw wisdom from the most unlikely places, such as fables and other stories and poems we learned in our youth. Examples include Aesop's "The Tortoise and the Hare" and "The Fox and the Stork" and many others that teach us valuable life lessons. These stories provide answers to survive through this financial crisis.

This reminds me of a poem I learned in high school. The poem narrates the story of a king who was ill and who could not be cured in spite of all the efforts and expensive medicine ordered from around the world. Finally a wise man recommends "the king will be well if he sleeps one night in the shirt of a happy (poor) man." How many of us would be so lucky to have been prescribed a simple medicine like that to cure our illnesses and shortcomings? We need constant reminders about the lessons of simplicity and contentment as displayed by Christ, Buddha, and Gandhi through their own lives. We cannot seem to grasp them well because we let our greediness, possessiveness, and false and fierce competition take over what is good in us. Every time we think we rose, we actually fell according to the higher order. We all need a periodic checkup of introspection and suggestions and advice from our mentors for proper direction.

How do we bring about the change we need to

improve our lives as well as of those living worlds away? Newspapers including *The New York Times, The Economist* and other regional and weekly papers do an admirable job of covering world events with in-depth studies of political, social, and economic conditions and history thereof through their coverage as well as special reports. There are also many publications available that share stories and opinions of experts, in various fields of national interest and foreign affairs. The X, Y, and Millennial generations are more comfortable educating themselves through the Internet and social media. Next, there has to occur an exchange of ideas and information that needs to get promoted in an unbiased fashion. We should not be afraid to express ourselves and share our thoughts and find out how others feel about those thoughts and ideas.

There is no magic formula to take care of all our problems because we will always be facing new ones. However, by taking a close look at history and delving into the lives of successful leaders, there are certain time tested theories and practices that can help us lead meaningful lives and equip us to deal with future problems and challenges as well. The following can help us achieve just that.

Simple living and happiness

Coming from a variety of economically diverse backgrounds, it is hard to define universally what simple living is; there are certain essential elements common to people from all economic strata that are easy to comprehend and practice. For example, we can all try to live a healthy life with an emphasis on natural hygiene and healthy food habits. The needs will vary from region to region within objective criteria. Local conditions, such as the weather, economic sustainability, and social environment, have an impact on what is considered a reasonable expectation of simple and healthy living. In order to achieve economic and social sustainability in the context of one's environment and surroundings, one must also be prepared to make mental adjustments and have realistic expectations of what is a good and affordable life. The mental discipline and practice of simple living helps individuals not to get tempted to go above and beyond what is sustainable for them. For example, businesses often promote deals that on the surface may seem attractive, but in the long run may prove unaffordable. Everyone needs to be educated enough to not fall victim to those types of deals. If they are not savvy enough to avoid these deals, which are constantly advertised through traditional media as well as social media, they need to find a trusted advisor.

Then there are those who are smart enough to apply their own austerity measures in putting their house in order, as narrated in *The New York Times* story on August 8, 2010. A California couple moved to Portland, Oregon, and changed their lifestyle drastically to rescue themselves from the shackles of high living and mounting debt. Inspired by books and blog entries, Tammy Strobel and her husband, Logan Smith, began getting rid of household items and even their two cars, eventually settling for a few necessities and a handful of things to fit in their 400 square feet studio apartment. They are now debt-free. She says, "I really believe that the acquisition of material goods doesn't bring about happiness." This is truly inspirational because we can also create our own story of survival and get out of our own circumstances.

Marshall Cohen, an analyst at the NPD Group, a retailing research and consulting firm, states, "we are moving from a conspicuous consumption—which 'is buy without regard'—to a calculated consumption." Ms. Strobel who now writes in her spare time says, "My lifestyle now would not be possible if I still had a huge two-bedroom apartment filled to the gills with stuff, two cars and $30 grand in debt....Give away some of your stuff and see how it feels," she advises.

Meanwhile, people who are up to their umpteenth million have increased their distance from the rest of the population. Being an accountant, I meet with people from all walks of life and income and wealth strata and help them manage their portfolios. There are many financial advisors and money managers will not even schedule a meeting with those whose wealth falls short of the high thresholds set by the advisors, which could be a multiple of many million dollars. How can these advisors understand the portfolios of the poor if they never help anyone without a portfolio worth millions of dollars?

Daryl Collins, Jonathan Morduch, Stuart Rutherford, and Orlanda Ruthven visited India, Bangladesh and South Africa and met with many poor people, compiled the book *Portfolios of The Poor: How The World's Poor Live on $2 a Day* from the financial diaries kept by those poor people. Thanks to their book, we can gain insight into how creative these people are in maintaining their daily affairs, and even saving from the meager earnings to build mini portfolios. They do not have to worry about maintaining thresholds or about banks rejecting their application because they did not have enough collateral. Many small entrepreneurs would not survive without microfinance, which supplements their other sources of finance such as loans from families, friends, neighbors, and employers. However, when they are able to scratch out a surplus, they also give out loans. Their portfolios are in single, double, or sometimes triple digits. The thousands are omitted because they do not exist. That is not a typo! They are micro money managers, except for them it's a daily activity without which survival would be impossible. The only thing that gets them going is hope and their ingenuity in managing their finances. This is done through a combination of daily savings of money and resources, borrowing, and utilizing the social networking. The hope is a big part of the equation not only for things to get better, but also expecting that a mother nature will be kind; therefore, they will have a better harvest, no floods, and no unforeseen tragedies that can wreck all plans. The rest of the world can become a bigger part of the solution if they speed up the spread of globalization, microfinance, and Millennium projects already on the ground so the bottom billion is pulled out of the trap and not left to do it all by themselves for thousands of years to come.

It is a lesson for all of us, whether in business or in a profession, to devote our attention to those who need our services or products but cannot afford to pay for them. As professionals, we should carve out part of our profits so our services and products can be made available to those who need them, either at discounted rates or gratis in acute cases. This opportunity may become available to us in our normal course of business, and also through our volunteer work. Some of my colleagues have chosen to serve only the nonprofit industry and focus all their energies toward social good. This dedication is very inspirational for us.

Here in the United States, it is a different story where a standard of living has crept up quite a bit. In the whole scheme of things, where does the middle class fit? They are not poor, yet they also do not have enough to realize all their dreams. Housing, tuition, transportation, and other mounting costs take a toll on middle class lives. It is a long, grueling marathon with no end in sight. How do we quantify this without worrying too much about inflation, which is still miniscule? Data suggest a family of four with school-age children can survive on $50,000 a year. Those with children attending college may have to go another notch (between $35,000 and $50,000) added for each child each year. This is where our choices for social programs and subsidized student loans become important in order to give the middle class a shot. A combination of smart public transportation availabilities and affordable housing will be needed to balance the equation so individual debts do not become unsustainable.

Education

Education is helpful in developing discipline in people to understand various forces, how they interact, and the delicate balance one must achieve to survive without causing economic and social hardship. Education gives us the confidence to not fall victim to the peer pressure of desiring material possessions and pursuing harmful activities. Ironically, assuming everything else is equal, education can give us the ability to live economically better lives, and partly reduce the inequality gap in our society. More importantly, though, education makes us feel good about ourselves and equips us with the ability to make better decisions. Along with our upbringing and environment, education helps us make the distinction between our wants and our needs. This is the key to literally bringing our houses in order.

Social activism and volunteerism

Higher education and being able to live a better life personally sometimes removes us from the daily grind of millions of people who are not so fortunate. Unfortunately society lauds individual successes and achievements above everything else. This encourages people to strive even harder to go to that next level of personal success and fortune building, and creates a peer pressure of a different kind, taking away one's ability to think independently, socially, and responsibly. Until we come to expect the rewards of higher education and training to benefit those in need, we are always going to fall behind in our perpetual quest for tangible social change. Think about the last social gathering you attended. You will notice those willing to help are the first ones to get up from their chairs, roll up their sleeves, and make the event enjoyable for all. These people do not need prompting, or titles, nor do they expect recognition. We need more people like that. These are the ones who have learned to live and enjoy life with others, rather than at their expense. These talents can be put to use at many social and nonprofit organizations in the area. They need volunteers to achieve, sustain, and further their causes. We should get involved whenever and wherever there is an opportunity and the need.

Connectivity

The problems of society and the world cannot be solved in a vacuum. We need to be connected to one another in meaningful ways, either through social media or in person. In order to achieve tangible results, this must occur constantly and effectively. No one in a free world is forced to honor these social obligations, therefore, they are difficult to implement. The only way it can be done is through individual efforts and involvement. One way to increase awareness early in our lives is through the establishment of mentor-mentee relationships with periodic evaluation and accountability. This two-way communication can be established at every stage of our development, in school, college, and even at work. That way it becomes part of everyone by establishing a positive reputation and an expectation of a moral obligation. Connectivity through communication becomes effective and can facilitate social change only if it is allowed to flow in all possible directions. Honesty, openness, and a willingness to change for the greater good are some of the essential elements that must be present for this communication to be effective.

At a global level, a worldview cannot be biased toward one group at the expense of another, no matter how established it might be in relation to the other due to their size, economic, and/or military superiority. The successes of nations and empires are not always a result of individual efforts; they may have a lot to do with their natural resources, or because of their geographical location and the climatic stability they came to enjoy over the centuries. It is therefore obligatory for these nations and empires to share their prosperity with geographically landlocked and strategically disadvantaged countries, and to become partners with them while also respecting their unique ways and customs, and understanding the tools they employ to sustain in the midst of their unique social, economic, political, and environmental conditions. It is hard to know how others live, and often we do not care because of this lack of understanding. We feel our lives are not even remotely affected by sad events occurring tens of thousands of miles away. Yes, we watch the news, and read about those events, but we rarely feel the pain of those personally affected by specific tragedies. It only becomes easier to relate to their pain when a similar tragedy befalls on us. We need to graduate from that stage and advance to a level where we are fully aware of the problems of others, even though things could be hunky-dory at home, and help those in distress through humanitarian efforts established by the international community, either through donations or by volunteering time.

The task to build our assets here and globally is perpetual. We will have to understand and agree as to what our individual and collective responsibility is to accomplish that task.

CHAPTER 6
Globalization

Migration is the oldest action against poverty, it selects those who most want help. It is good for the country to which they go; it helps break the equilibrium of poverty in the country from which they come. What is the perversity in the human soul that causes people to resist so obvious a good?

John Kenneth Galbraith
American Statesman and Economist

Globalization in some form or the other has always existed in the civilized world, but its realization gained momentum with the advent of the Internet and e-commerce. More and more businesses and start-ups involve multiple countries because of the entrepreneurial spirit of the X and Y generations, the availability of super speed Internet, and consequently easy accessibility of services and products. In its most advanced stage, the data are now accessed through cloud technology rather than the traditional transmittal, with an eye on cost cutting, convenience, and speed.

Yet this modernization is still in its infancy, both in terms of its technical advancement and usage, which is far from universal. In addition, one must be aware of the cultural differences in constituent countries, language barriers, and international trade restrictions, sanctions, and protocols.

The latest financial crisis forced many

countries to take a protectionist attitude toward foreign trade, outsourcing, and immigration issues. Many countries are still working to resolve many of these issues as they are slowly coming out of recession. For example, in Greece, Spain, and some mid-eastern countries, the unemployment rates are around 25%, which certainly affect outsourcing, immigration, emigration, out-shoring, and in-shoring of jobs. Even where the unemployment rates are not as high, but still in high single digits, the same problems remain.

Once people gain more confidence both about their ability to succeed and about the overall business environment, they must try to pursue partnerships with their counterparts abroad where it makes sense. Governments should support internationalization of trade and business without being overly concerned about loss of jobs at home. The problem of jobs cannot be solved in a vacuum. Job creation is a joint task of business people, governments, and workers. It requires creativity and flexibility on the part of businesses and new workers, both as to the nature of jobs and the working conditions. The possibility of remote access adds convenience both for employers and employees with the resultant cost benefit by creation of "virtual business arrangements." The globalization of trade and business thrives on these virtual stations and super connectivity.

The issue of establishing a nexus for taxing revenues is always a part of the discussion and must be addressed by all the countries involved in cooperation with one another. The issue of taxing multinationals on their worldwide income is being dealt with as part of tax reform and will have an impact on how those multinationals and those who generate revenue worldwide will do business. Tax treaties and tax rates in different countries will have an impact on planning and putting together deals. National governments are currently in the process of seeking cooperation from international banks as to the disclosures with respect to the offshore funds deposited with them.

If removing poverty and inequality from the face of the earth is our top priority, then we all must work together and look at the problem globally and not just from a domestic perspective. Philippe Legrain illustrates this in his book, *Immigrants: Your Country Needs Them*. He says if you think about it, a Mexican waiter offering his services in the United States is no different from an American banker offering his services in London or Mexico City. Change is never easy, both in perception and in real feasible terms, because people, just like governments and institutions, do not like to break away from the old norms, but need to for long term sustainability. Our institutions must do a good job of understanding this and then educating people to make business decisions in an unbiased manner. International and local laws dealing with human rights issues need to be honored and applied without discrimination. The focus must shift to prevention through education.

Immigration and globalization

Let us hope immigration reform is comprehensive when passed. It must assure the reunion of thousands of families who are living apart, including minors apart from their parents, due to deportation and harsh residency provisions. The law must also provide protection to those who are being taken advantage of by employers due to their uncertain residency status, language barriers and economic conditions. Minimum wages and regular wages should be enforced so there is equal pay for everyone for the same job. The same must hold true for overtime worked. One must understand that immigrants, irrespective of their status, are just like the rest of us with realistic expectations for their efforts and aspirations to do better. Wait at the street corner every morning in Main Street America, and you will see truckloads of young children boarding school buses hoping to change their lives. This, thanks to their parents who are doing two, sometimes three jobs, so their children get the best education and hopefully live better lives than they did. It is our obligation to notice all this and do all we can to make it happen for those hard-working individuals.

For those *disillusioned* about the benefits of being an American, we must educate them and draw a roadmap for them to understand sacrifices one must make to earn citizenship. This would be achieved by learning, educating, and becoming assets to this society. Some of them have done just that. Against all odds they have become representatives at the local and national level and some in exceptional cases have found a seat on the highest court in the country. At this rate, it is conceivable to expect one day this country will be led by one of those aspiring and *deserving* immigrants. The success and presence of all immigrants is validated mostly by their educational and professional excellence, especially when they come from foreign cultural backgrounds, with different languages and even physical characteristics. It takes a lot of courage and determination in order for immigrants to succeed and eventually be accepted by those who preceded them. The process of Americanization has a price tag attached to it. They must overcome humiliation and discrimination (both blatant and subtle), but in the end it is all worth it and sweeter when they are accepted as Americans. Interesting enough, America becomes richer in a diverse culture and languages, with a breadth of social and moral values and diverse economic *ways* through this process of immigration and *integration.*

In that regard, America is a worthy candidate to promote and practice globalization. In the harmonious human society without borders, does it really matter whether you are called a developed or emerging or an undeveloped country? Each is only a stage through which every country passes on its way to prosperity. Globalization ought to make that possible for those left behind so they also can join the party. The heart of globalization efforts should be worker empowerment so they feel part of the success and growth, instead of feeling used and abused in the name of cost cutting. When I look at the label on my shirt and see it was made abroad in India, China, Bangladesh, Viet Nam, or Sri Lanka, I think of the nameless worker who stitched my shirt and the delicate hands of some unknown lady or a teenager who sewed buttons on it. I often wonder how they must be living and how they must be feeling about their roles in world trade and the impact they make in the lives of people thousands of miles away. If a meeting was a success, or if one finds a dream job that one was hoping to get, then that unknown worker who put your shirt together also shares in that success, whether or not he or she knows it. My only hope is, and therefore I want a promise from the seller, the maker of my shirt was properly compensated and was provided with adequate working conditions and treated with respect!

As outlined in Chapter 2, multilateral organizations, national governments, NGOs, and nonprofit organizations have a positive role to play in promoting globalization. Each of these types of organizations brings its unique abilities and position on the world stage to help businesses and social organizations in education, training, and even providing resources that make globalization possible. The businesses with a profit motive are already operating at an international level through their network of companies and subsidiaries and contribute significantly toward increasing global wealth. The area that needs to develop both domestically and internationally, though, is social business.

Social Business and microfinance

As mentioned earlier, Yunus and others work tirelessly to promote microfinance and social business. Without microfinance, millions of disadvantaged people would still be poor. Without social businesses, many would still be deprived of basic necessities and opportunities to work productively. These programs are not meant just to benefit the local economy, but they need to be translated into global networks through which all aspiring entrepreneurs can benefit in promoting trade and commerce.

Microfinance brings bank services to the poor at conditions affordable to them, as opposed to going to the banks on the banks' terms. As suggested by the proponents of microfinance and social businesses, the indigenous bank structure is for marginal and small start-up businesses for its easy access, operating simplicity, and community involvement. The underlying principle in establishing microfinance is to make credit available to those who could not qualify and afford to borrow under conventional banking systems.

This type of arrangement requires the support of private individuals, local business communities, governments, and regulatory agencies. Coupled with this, there must exist business and consumer friendly trade policies to promote foreign trade across borders, which would further ensure global social and economic progress. The government, regulatory, and trade agencies, in addition to oversight and compliance, must provide training and guidance in fair global trade so those not familiar with the culture and business practices in foreign countries do not fall victim to corruption and shortchanging. Yunus, envisions a social stock market dealing in securities of social businesses. This will require a whole new terminology, literature, education, and even regulatory bodies and social credit agencies to rate the capital issues of social businesses. This is where my concept of recognizing and measuring social net worth, highlighted in Chapter 5, will come into play. These are the ideas that need enough traction for them to turn into action and eventually sustain themselves. We need people to adopt and embrace these ideas even though they may have been conceived by someone else.

Education

Education, both academic and vocational, is vital in promoting global trade. The Internet has proven to be a useful tool by making a wealth of data and information available for anyone planning a business venture.

However, formal and authoritative education and training at conventional institutions and online courses are still needed to ensure those who pursue global trade are knowledgeable and competent to trade and enter into contracts. In addition, an education in international economics and knowledge about the cultures, languages, and political systems of different countries are important for successful global trading. Global conferences, seminars, and trade shows should provide access to knowledge about technologies, innovations, and prevailing business practices and environment around the globe. As advertised in trade magazines, there are a number of courses available and scores of conferences conducted every year dealing with these issues, but often their costs are prohibitive, beyond the reach of many. This specialized knowledge through education needs to be available at affordable rates in order to benefit a larger audience and create equal business opportunities.

Whether or not we like it, globalization is here to stay and is the new wave on which ideas, opinions, trades, and establishment of social and business relationships will ride. It is, therefore, very important we quickly understand the various elements and dynamics that make globalization possible and practice it so everyone benefits.

Chapter 7
Creating a Legacy

Don't judge each day by the harvest you reap, but by the seeds that you plant.

Robert Louis Stevenson
Scottish Novelist, Poet, and Essayist

At some point, everyone must step back and give serious thought to his or her legacy and contribute value to this world that will be remembered and treasured a long time. Some by their nature and their dealings are already making a positive contribution to the world.

Along life's journey, our contacts and rich experiences give us inspiration to build our own legacy. There are many examples of great people who have made a universal impact and continue to enjoy the respect of the multitudes for generations and way past their lives. For example, there is Buddha, who after 2,500 years still inspires millions to understand and practice simple living and spiritual and selfless thinking. Gandhi, who followed a path of nonviolence and Satyagraha, continues to inspire millions of people to practice his ways to fight for equality and justice. Our Founding Fathers had a big and profound vision, the light of which created a nation the rest of the world is proud of, looks up to, and tries to emulate. There are also ordinary heroes who laid down their lives to defend their countries, and scientists and inventors who burned the midnight oil to bring light to the world. Let us not forget writers and teachers who inspire us to be creative and help us deal with our lives as best as we could, and unsung heroes and people who help us get through our daily grind; even if we do not know or remember their names, they still count. Each one of us must dig deep into our hearts to find the rare qualities we possess, to follow our passion and instincts, and to pursue those unique tasks and not to be afraid of failing or being ridiculed. The more difficult the path, the uncertainty of direction and terrain, the more compelling it is to pursue that journey.

There are many examples of explorers and brave men who, against all odds, achieved something no one else before them even thought about. Columbus was originally headed for India or the Far East, but instead landed on an unknown land mass, a discovery that would benefit generations to come. Vasco Da Gama, in his travels, endured a few more days of suspense and uncertainty while passing through the Cape of Good Hope at the southernmost tip of Africa, thus turning the corner before ultimately reaching India, in search of goods and trade. There is a brave act out there for all of us with our name written all over it, ready to be found and explored from which the whole humanity can benefit. It may not be extraordinary, it may only impact a few, but it does count. This may be your "Aha" moment, during an otherwise dull meeting, or your instinct to save a drowning kid at a local pool, or save a neighbor's cat—random acts, but good, life-changing and life-saving ones that count. Some among us do just that, like that business executive and a member of the local Chamber of Commerce who pledged and successfully honored 50 deeds in a single year in which he turned fifty years old.

Every year, a dozen Nobel prizes are given out in the fields of science, economics, literature, and peace to those who worked hard for years, persevered, and excelled in their field of expertise. We can find inspiration and something of value that would benefit all of humanity from those people. The peace efforts must continue beyond these ceremonial recognitions, as was expressed by Martti Ahtisarri, a former President of Finland (1994-2000) and the 2008 Nobel Prize winner in peace. He said, "Peace is such an essential and desirable element and state in our lives that we should achieve, attain, and preserve it without much fuss and ado." One day someone will come up with a brilliant plan to resolve the disputes across, the Middle East, Far East, and Africa to bring peace and equality around the globe.

It puzzles me there are those who commit mass murders and show no remorse also have families and love their children, parents, brothers, sisters, and spouses, yet what is it that makes them behave differently with others? Is it because of different beliefs and prejudices? What can we do to change that? What are their expectations of the world that could bring about peace and harmony? Finding answers and solutions that can change the world forever should be our legacy-in-common.

I mentioned earlier we are all shaped in the same mold and are expected to work toward individual goals so we can ultimately achieve financial security for ourselves. There is nothing wrong with those goals, and it requires great efforts to achieve that. In a perfect world, that simple equation would make everyone happy and prosperous. Unfortunately it does not always work out that way. This is because we are so preoccupied with improving our own lives and would do anything to not jeopardize it, that we end up ignoring our obligations to create a common good. This madness and obsession with individual success at any cost has widened the gap between the haves and have nots with economic and social consequences. This ultimately leads to global conflicts, both big and small. Generations from now, we want to be remembered as people who cared, who worked hard to bring peace and harmony among all nations, and who worked together to keep our planet sustainable. We need to break from the ranks to create good norms, the foundation upon which the future generations will be able to create their own legacies.

We need to change the way we think, the way we deal with people, and learn to question the status quo when it fails to achieve what it was instituted for. It is inherent in all human nature to become comfortable in our surroundings and, therefore, guard it at any cost. This hinders evolution and progress and makes adaptation to new surroundings and circumstances difficult to breed. We must fight to remain alert and look for opportunities for change. We must truly become a global community by having an understanding of everything around us, peoples and places, near and far, and make all concerns our own, without which no change will ever occur.

In order to become meaningful, our institutions must change and evolve. Their ultimate success will be measured in terms of the quality and the extent of services they provide and not by their size and the material progress they make. Similarly, for the people who are working in these institutions, their progress will be measured by their contribution toward a common good and not by their mere adherence to internal bureaucracy. Our political institutions must flourish to respect, honor, and protect all humane ideologies without bias so society can make a true progress.

When our children look up to celebrities and try to follow in their footsteps, we must point out the sacrifices they made on the way to realizing their dreams, instead of simply focusing on the tangible benefits and comforts that came with their success. Our children should look at the social involvement and the causes these celebrities promote. When we wear the hats and tee-shirts of our favorite teams and our stars, it reminds us of their greatness, their achievements, and thereby become part of their glory. It is not easy to be worthy of the legacies these heroes leave behind. What happens on that playground or field is created from scratch with human determination, and a lot of pride. While becoming a witness to the living history, there is also an opportunity to take a pointer or two from the whole experience for our "next at bat." All my life I have been blessed with freedom to think and do as I please. I have had rich experiences and have been encouraged to strive for more. I am glad to share my experiences and thoughts with you, which may become helpful to you in your next at bat!

I am reminded of the final scene in the movie, *Mr. Deeds*, starring Adam Sandler. He asks everyone in the audience what they wished to become when they were growing up, and what they ultimately ended up becoming. Most confessed they did not realize their childhood dreams or even a spirit underlying their dreams that could identify with their wish. Most of us end up that way because either we do not work hard enough or with a passion to realize those dreams, or we succumb to the pressures of the time, which take us away from our mission. In essence, we become part of the herd led by others. Do not let that be your fate! We must fight this herd mentality and listen to our hearts and channel our energies in achieving our childhood dreams in spite of the hurdles.

When I was young, I was obsessed with cricket, the national passtime in India, just like baseball is here in America. A woman once asked me what I was good at: batting, bowling, fielding, or catching. I told her I was an all-rounder meaning good in all aspects of cricket: batting, bowling, fielding, catching, and even captaining. Months later, she presented me with a cricket book with the inscription "To an all-rounder," on the first page. I never became a cricketer, but the well-roundedness in me helped me pursue everything in life with total devotion and an appreciation for all aspects of life's tasks. I have accepted my career changes and many roles with open arms, and despite the challenges I faced, I brought enough sincerity to make them work. Famous baseball celebrity Yogi Berra once said, "When you come to a fork in the road, take it." He always had a funny way of saying things that had a lot of truth in it and it went straight to your heart.

From my early days, I have taken very seriously what was taught to me at school and at home. Even at an early age, I could see the distinction between what I was taught and how it played out in the street and in real life. I had to decide quickly to which world I wanted to belong. Even at that tender age, there was a price to be paid for having chosen the life of the righteous. I parted with some very close friends because I knew then our paths would never converge and it would be even tougher to part with them later on had I continued my association with them. In that challenging environment, I must say with some pride, there was a humanity of friends who supported my views and my way of life. To this day some of them admire my courage to have chosen well. Even the so-called school bullies melted when confronting me because they held me to a different standard and knew deep down they were wrong. In that regard, I felt rewarded for bringing about a change in their behavior and finally realizing what is appropriate behavior. My following the likes of Gandhi, and other household heroes, earned me the respect not only of my peers, but the teachers as well, who were openly partial toward me and let others know why that act of discrimination was justified.

Therefore, a strong foundation of character is so important to withstand other similar or even more comprehensive battles of principles in the future. You never know who your real friends are, who follow your life so closely and admire you for being role models to them. It can take a lifetime to figure that out. Even after you are gone, the light will keep shining as I witnessed when my father passed away. I saw admiration and sorrow in the eyes of hundreds who gathered to pay their respects and again at the prayer meeting a few days after the funeral. I saw the same spectacle of pouring emotions again at my mother's passing. There is consolation even as these noble souls moved on; they left behind a precious legacy and endless possibilities for thousands they came in contact with during their lives.

The great thing about being on this earth is to have freedom to dream things that are achievable as well as the wild and impossible. The tangibles are there for all to see, but it is the intangibles which make life interesting and enjoyable. The intangibles tickle your heart and brains, and if allowed to nurture, they become raw material from which great legends are born.

CHAPTER 8
Think Outside the Box

A desk is a dangerous place from which to view the world.

John Le Carre, English Author

The world is a better place today than it was centuries ago, all made possible through the efforts of those who thought outside the box. This requires a lot of courage and willingness to risk everything. Unfortunately, average human beings have a tendency to think and act in herds. We are afraid to try new ways and continue to protect the status quo within and stay within our comfort zones. German-American psychologist Erich Fromm observed, "Creativity requires the courage to let go of certainties." Without trying, you will never discover your true potential and strengths.

Some are born free, and we see them among us in all walks of life, for example, entrepreneurs who possess rare qualities which make them move faster to cut through the maze and eventually succeed. Those with courage may take a leap of faith and jump in the pool without gauging the depth and worrying about the chill in the water. Most people, though, are cautious but they can at least inquire of those who have already plunged as to the depth and the temperature and feel the water with their toe first before jumping into it.

This art and practice of "thinking outside the box" also helps deal with unforeseen crises later in life. The mind, now trained to think in the midst of uncertainty, will look for parallels in other areas of life to find solutions and ways to deal with the problem at hand. The trained mind will learn and become good at either accepting or rejecting competing ideas. That is why this is such an important quality to possess and develop. This quality was shared by both Warren Buffet and the late Steve Jobs, and it helped put them at the pinnacle of their careers.

In my case, the sabbatical helped me unwind, clear my head, and look at my career as an accountant from the outside. The sabbatical became a bridge to get me through new territory—the financial crisis of 2008 and its aftermath. These posed challenges, but at the same time provided opportunities to find new ways to lead us all out of the morass.

Thinking outside the box is a priceless pursuit to improve one's lot and change one's surrounding. Obviously one must focus on one's strengths before taking the leap of faith. Judy Garland, the American actress and singer, said, "Always be a first rate version of yourself, instead of a second rate version of somebody else." Further, not every action can be initiated or performed by a single individual. Some tasks require collective efforts. Without kingmakers there are no kings, and there are no leaders without their supporters. I recently stumbled upon an article on the Internet, "The 50 Most Innovative Companies, and the Attributes That Set Them

Apart," by Neil Amato, published on November 4, 2013. The companies he mentions have integrated innovation into their corporate culture and, as a result, have had phenomenal success.

We have been blessed with centuries of world leaders, spiritual leaders, and thinkers: Jesus Christ, Buddha, Muhammad, Moses, the Dalai Lama, Mohandas Gandhi, Benjamin Franklin, George Washington, Napoleon Bonaparte, Aristotle, Martin Luther King, Jr., Confucius, Nelson Mandela, Albert Einstein, Sir Isaac Newton, Thomas Alva Edison, Louis Pasteur, Madame Curie, and many others. They all displayed remarkable qualities of perseverance, patience, sacrifice, vision, and a sense of responsibility. Above all, they had the ability to step away from their charted route to achieve something extraordinary to benefit the whole humanity.

Institutions all over the world are already moving to include the art of critical thinking skills in school curriculums, to better prepare the next generation to face the challenges ahead. This becomes even more important in an increasingly borderless world. It is time to shed age-old customs and rituals and give way to new ideas where international brotherhood can breed and blossom. In addition to the traditional ranking criteria for the nation's colleges, they are now also graded on the value they generate relative to the underlying cost involved. While it is still necessary to offer courses that prepare graduates in technical areas, some institutions have shifted their focus to humanities and economics in order to prepare socially conscious individuals. We are already seeing a massive increase in start-up organizations by students even before they graduate; that is how the younger generation thinks. Their survival, though, hinges on the positive social footprint they will generate. The proof is beyond the tee-shirts they wear labeling the social causes they stand for.

Sometimes older ideas or laws may need to be reinvented to solve crises, as is being practiced by federal prosecutors in dealing with cases involving financial irregularities and mortgage frauds perpetrated during the recent crisis. The old law that found favor with the prosecutors is the Financial Institutions Reform, Recovery, and Enforcement Act (FIRREA), which because it is a civil statute, and requires a lower burden of proof than criminal charges—finding guilt by a preponderance of the evidence versus the beyond a reasonable doubt theory, as reported in *The New York Times* article on October 31, 2013. Thanks to these smart lawyers for their wisdom and curiosity to bring justice.

Like I mentioned earlier, human beings think and act in herds, either by nature but mostly because of the necessity to survive. Largely workers are affiliated with institutions and feel obligated to be loyal to them and not question their actions. It is hard for individuals to cut through the bureaucracy and stand up for their beliefs. However, it is important to take necessary action whenever justified, to improve working conditions, and make a positive social impact. If the organization is sensitive to changes and new ideas, the task becomes that much easier. When there is resistance to change, though, it becomes difficult to operate in that environment and may even compel one to leave the organization. This may not always be the best option as it disrupts the workflow, careers, prove to be inefficient, and will have an impact on morale within the organization. The answer lies in following the right path, by building alliances from day one, convincing people through persuasion, and setting an example.

Everyone needs someone they can trust to share their ideas and doubts with without fear of being ridiculed. We need to go even further and question those we look up to if we want to see real change. Again the golden words of Buddha teach us better in *Coffee with The Buddha*, by Joan Oliver:

"Do not place blind trust in impressive personalities or venerated gurus, but examine the issue for yourselves. When you know for yourselves that something is wholesome and beneficial, then you should accept it and put it in practice. Ultimately even the teachings had to be set aside, once they had served the purpose. Think of the dharma (religion) as a raft. You use it to transport yourself across the river, but when you are safely on the other shore, you set it down, you don't carry it with you. After you have reached Nirvana (salvation), what need do you have for a raft?"

One must seek those who promote new ideas, are willing to try new ways, share them with others, and spread them through media. It helps to get in the debate about ideas with your friends, family, colleagues, and even strangers. An encounter with a stranger can either be akin to striking a gold mine or it might prove to be a total disaster depending on which side of the bed you woke up that morning. If it happens to be your lucky day, it opens up possibilities you never dreamed of before. Here's why: Because the stranger never knew who you were, where you came from, or what your affiliations were, he brings to the table fresh and unbiased ideas and opinions that when combined with your ideas and opinions brought out during the debate, creates a healthy amalgam to change the world.

The Millennial Generation seems comfortable thinking outside the box all the time. Tom Agan, co-founder of Rivia, an innovation and brand consulting firm, in his article, "Embracing the Millennials," in *The New York Times* on November 10, 2013, talks about how some companies have recognized this new group as game changers and urges the mainstream corporate world to integrate them in the decision-making process. In fact, the very makeup of the Millennial Generation cries out for innovation, transparency, and instant communication through technology. They do not need to learn to think outside the box. Being an outlier is more a norm than a rarity for them, and they feel quite comfortable operating and achieving goals without titles and accolades.

We are becoming a borderless society, well-informed and transparent, thanks to unfettered communication. With that the demographics are also changing gradually in favor of the younger generation who has a knack for drawing necessary lessons from its present surroundings without becoming too emotionally and politically attached. In the light of this optimistic promise offered by this new generation, one wishes the world to become a safer and more open place for everyone and that the world engages in a healthy education and knowledge race rather than the arms race. Then and then only will we have learned the true significance of the United Nations and its spirit.

Chapter 9
The Future

I ask not for a lighter burden, but for broader shoulders.

- Jewish Proverb

This chapter is dedicated to the Millennial Generation, but also encourages discussion that benefit all generations. This takes me back to the future I envisioned way back, long before I entered adulthood and faced the hard realities of life and the world around me. I want the current generation to know my generation went through what they are going through now—lots of questions with very few answers. The times and events of each generation dictate what those expectations turn out to be.

In stark contrast to what I experienced growing up, I am proud to state the new generation seems to have a spirit strong enough to deal with the present and is also preparing quite well to deal with the uncertainties of the future. Having said that, my generation has the obligation to set a strong foundation upon which the future generations can build their dreams, and alert them to the inherent dangers and difficulties in the growing process. More importantly, we need to bridge communication gaps between the generations in terms of expectations of each other.

I must admit, just like many who in their prime years spend a disproportionate amount of time at work and, therefore, failed to connect with their children, I, too, have been guilty. Our children may have unanswered questions and doubts about many things that could have been resolved if only we kept that line of communication open all the time. I envy those who can fulfill that responsibility to their heart's content. In my case, my wife stepped in to play the dual role of being a working mother and raising children. As is evident from their behavior, she has done a great job.

Outside of our personal lives and relationships, there are things such as world affairs that must always be addressed in today's global environment. There are innumerable issues which ultimately decide the fate of our children: Schooling, community involvement, internships, the many interests they pursue or dream about all have a deep impact in shaping their future and the future of the world around them. Within education there are arguments for and against home schooling, and tough decisions to be made striking the right balance between core education, extracurricular activities, and the role of sports and entertainment in their lives. These ongoing issues must be constantly evaluated and acted upon. More importantly, though, the ground needs to be made suitable for the young graduates to enter the real world, a terrain they are totally unfamiliar with. They are watching and making their own conclusions and unless we make a conscious effort to stay with our children during that realization process, they will make wrong assumptions and draw wrong conclusions and that will not be pretty. It is the responsibility of parents, teachers, and mentors of this generation to create a strong present so that the next generation's backbone becomes stronger than its wishbone.

Despite being at the top of my class for most of my school years and being labeled an ideal and diligent student, I was always a proponent for home schooling. My beliefs were influenced by that great soul Rabindranath Tagore, who in 1913 became the first non-European to win the Nobel Prize in Literature for his collection of poems, *Gitanjali.* Tagore later founded an institution in a quaint setting that the world knows as "Shantiniketan" (the closest meaning is where peace resides), a distinguished institution. India's late Prime Minister Indira Gandhi and Amartya Sen, a Nobel Laureate in economics, were among the leaders who spent part of their careers there. My personal preference for home schooling, a wish never granted to me, was the idea of being educated in an unrestrained environment, not tied to a rigid regimen, and learning whatever your heart desired, whenever you felt like it. I later came to realize that with freedom comes responsibility one can never afford to ignore, because in the end you have to make sure society benefits from your efforts, no matter the mode of your education.

The challenge of choosing a career is larger than most students realize. Many students do not know what they want to graduate in or their strengths. The advice they receive from counselors and parents is sometimes biased. Some parents want their children to accomplish their own dreams that remained unfulfilled because of their circumstances.

The recent economic crisis has made this process even more challenging because it has made it difficult for parents to grant their children their wishes, from choosing the summer camps they would love to attend with their friends to possessing the latest technologically advanced mobile device to the ultimate dream of attending their first choice college. Sometimes these dreams cannot be fulfilled because they are unaffordable.

For most of us, these are trying times. Affordable housing, affordable transportation, affordable education, and affordable health care are issues the resolution of which will determine the success of the current generation and create a roadmap for the future to follow. This needs to get accomplished urgently, by resolving the differences between different ideologies, priorities, and visions.

Here in America many still cannot afford what is realistically achievable, yet there are a fortunate few who easily enjoy luxury and social advantages, without any worries. It cannot be that difficult to bring equality in opportunity and just rewards for hard work and personal sacrifices when we are quite rich in the overall resources available and at our disposal, both physical and intellectual. Recently the American working class (especially fast food workers, mostly young people starting out), with the help of Fast Food Forward and Fight for 15 (FFF) Campaigns, organized strikes to make audible their demand for an increase in the minimum wage. FFF was launched by the Service Employees International Union (SEIU) in 2012, advancing efforts to pressure employers to raise wages and benefits for low wage employees. These workers are also inspired by the Occupy Wall Street (OWS) movement, which was a protest movement that began on September 17, 2011, in New York City's financial district. The main issues raised by OWS were social and economic inequality, greed, corruption, and the perceived undue influence of corporations on government. The methods used by OWS were occupation, civil disobedience, picketing, demonstrations, and Internet activism. A decent wage helps our neighbors, improves our own lot, and creates a safe and homogeneous society.

If Gandhi was not afraid to try his innovative ways of nonviolence, noncooperation movement to shake the mighty British Empire and eventually make them see the wisdom in relinquishing their control on India, why can't we Americans apply the same principles of that noncooperation movement by staging hunger strikes, agitation, and boycott, against the institutions in our own communities that operate to further their self-interests without regard to economic and social consequences caused to others? In a democracy, the socioeconomic reforms must originate at the grassroots level but it sure helps if they are supported by the Government policies that promote those reforms. If we silently succumb to rising costs of necessities, and yes, education is one of them, the inequality will widen and young students will be forced to pursue below par education, or be deprived of higher education altogether and create a weak and ill-prepared workforce in the process, not to mention the social upheaval this may create. On a global scale, this could make it very hard for our youth to compete, thus further hindering their progress.

We must act in a timely manner so it does not come to that. We are the melting pot and the envy of the world. We need to rekindle our spirit to make sure that we remain the guiding star for the rest of the world to follow.

America has provided so much for so many that the possibilities are limitless. Let us share our good fortunes and prosperity with our counterparts around the globe. Let that be the lesson for the future generations! Let them see the connection between us and the rest of the world, to let them see the sacrifices their fathers and forefathers endured to make it in this Promised Land, and let them appreciate everything they have and understand the price paid by many so ***they*** are able to enjoy the fruits.

As for affordable education, some states have already taken the initiative and suggested college costs can be brought down as low as $10,000 for a four-year degree. This may involve a combination of four-year college, using online courses followed by competency exams, and partnering with local community colleges where students spend one or two years prior to transferring to four-year institutions. This also reduces ever-mounting student loans. Texas government called for such plans for Texas universities in 2011, which have been adopted by over a dozen Texas public universities. Florida and California have also urged the public universities in their states to limit undergraduate education to $10,000. In February 2014, Tennessee Gov. Bill Haslam proposed to waive tuition for students at community colleges and technology centers. Tennessee would create an endowment fund from the Tennessee Education Lottery to cover tuition and fees. Several states including Arkansas, Georgia, and South Carolina use lottery money to provide merit based scholarships. Students themselves are creative in bringing down the mounting cost of education by signing up for online courses and taking the College Level Examination Program (CLEP) tests.

There are, however, critics of these plans who think they are political gimmicks. Private schools argue if these bold plans can guarantee the same quality of education that the elite schools provide. The current state of the economy has hurt all of us, including pricey institutions. That's why the Governor of Massachusetts's 2007 proposal to offer free community college education lost steam. The truth is we lack political and social courage to implement such programs, which make more sense in these uncertain times than ever before in our nation's history. The message needs to be spread across the nation. All institutions must look closely at their budgets and make the necessary sacrifices for it to happen. We need a comprehensive reform in which everyone makes sacrifices in order to make the whole system work. The education reform should be part of the overall change that would guarantee equality of lifestyles and opportunities.

The other very important aspect of education reform deals with the quality of education itself. In this regard, there are already good ideas promoted by organizations such as Teach for America (TFA), The New Teacher Project (TNTP), and similar bodies trying to improve the quality of education by improving the lot of teachers. The certification, advancement, and survival of teachers must depend on their merits rather than their tenure. Under such programs, teachers are screened comprehensively at the interview stage and are subject to constant evaluation both onsite and offsite, which helps retain the best teachers in the system. More Millennials are pursuing this noble career, foregoing other more lucrative careers. Our nation's governments and institutions must continue to invest in the education reform to make their efforts worth their while, as the Millennials are helping build stronger and better educated future graduates and workforce. Sadly, there is not enough lobbying to legislate the reforms in education that are vital to our future growth.

The length, breadth, and nature of education must be such that we produce graduates who are well-rounded in many disciplines and equipped to face the challenges of tomorrow with a spirit of cooperation and understanding. Tomorrow's leaders will be picked by consensus, their inclusive spirit, and mutual respect rather than by opportunistic means. They will be led by the issues at hand rather than by their narrow agenda and party lines. Politics will again assume its role as an art in diplomacy, rather than a dirty word used only to signify assumption and perpetuity of power.

The present generation needs to understand the generations that follow, their dreams, habits, body language, and the way they operate and facilitate communication. Those at the helm of major organizations are already making necessary adjustments in the way they operate and communicate to make it workable for new hires. The work culture must also ensure that businesses and their clients are also in sync with this new order to achieve efficiencies. Work/life balance and flexible schedules are already integrated at many institutions to improve morale, creativity, and productivity, as well as longevity. Smaller outfits, such as traditional mom and pop businesses, must follow suit if they want to survive the competition. The traditional corporate hierarchy must be replaced with a more integrated workforce and open work stations with free flow of ideas. *That* will be the norm that will measure success.

Today's youth are engaged from day one and conduct adequate research before their first interview. They are as much interested in finding out what they will get out of the arrangement in terms of nurturing their intellectual skills, anticipated career path, and social environment, as much as their commitment to make valuable contributions. Today's youth thrives on two-way communication and will not stop at anything to find things out and to figure things out. We need to sit down with them, if you can pin them down, and emphasize the importance of slowing down a little, perhaps do in-depth research and study of a subject or two rather than constantly looking for easy and short answers just to solve the problem at hand. For our part, we need to create an ideal space and environment for them to grow whole-heartedly. We as parents, teachers, and employers have to be sensitive to their needs to assure intended consequences.

From day one, we should provide the open environment in which they can interact with their peers at home, but also understand and stay connected with their counterparts in far-off places. For example, many years ago my daughter, through a Christian Fund, donated $24 a month to help pay for the elementary school education of a young girl in India. Then there are high school juniors and seniors who pursue humanitarian deeds like those high school kids from Princeton High who raised enough money to bore water wells in remote parts of the world. Every year thousands of Peace Corps volunteers spend their time and efforts around the globe helping others with education, farming, and hygiene and achieving their basic needs. Through organizations such as Doctors Without Borders, there are doctors who give their valuable expertise and service.

Ideally the next generation will be so engaged on a routine basis without much fuss or ado. They will not have to wait decades to earn a merit like the Nobel award for their life changing contributions because, for them, it will be a norm to be constantly engaged in noble causes. They may not only carry the logo "world peace and prosperity" on their tee-shirts, but their DNA will reflect it at all times as well.

Today's youth face many challenges upon entering the workforce. In my field, for example, the biggest task any graduate entering the profession of accounting is to try to apply the principles he or she learned to real-life situations and work. To make matters worse, one must also try to understand and deliver what is expected of them at every level of the professional ladder they will ascend. There will be a constant struggle between acting on the superior's orders and acting on one's own conscience and to overcome that dilemma in the light of moral and professional ethics. There will be friends to be made, professional relationships to be developed and nurtured, mentors to be found, and mentees to be groomed, leadership opportunities to be explored, and contributions to be made in furthering the prospect and respect of the profession. I guarantee this will not be easy knowing the nature of the beast; it is likely in the process, friendships will be jeopardized and professional relationships will be made or broken based on personal views. One will be at the crossroads of professional choices and options, more than they bargained for when entering the accounting profession. There will be times when one hates it all, and at other times one will love every moment of it. In the end, by doing the right thing and respecting human values, one becomes a better professional, and even a better person. The accounting profession provides that unique opportunity to do good because it teaches one to be ethical, transparent, accountable, and instills in one a healthy skepticism to not fall asleep at the wheel. Success is also measured by one's adherence to these qualities and attributes. The rest does not matter. Big and small firms must always promote the best practices and forego financial gains if the means in attaining them are tainted. Every morning we, as accountants, need to remind ourselves "we are independent and professionals first" and will proceed through our day's mission with that thought firmly grounded in our minds.

Just like others, accounting professionals also need annual checkups. We have to continue to act in a way that assures a healthy environment for new prospects, as well as for those who have invested their lives in servicing this profession, and to make sure accountants always act so that all the stakeholders can rely on our professional opinions in basing their business decisions. We are advocates for our clients, but only when they are worthy of the legal or professional recourse necessary to achieve justice, and not when their objectives violate public policy and ethics. At such times we may be forced to sever our relationships with them, however lucrative it may be. One way to overcome this catastrophe would be to screen the prospective clients at the outset and determine before they come aboard whether they are a right fit. Younger generations will look toward our actions and seek guidance when they confront a situation involving conflict of interest and ethics. We must, as a profession, be united in these efforts.

I am sure the same holds true for other professions, such as medicine, law, engineering, and other social sciences. No matter which profession you belong to, your strong DNA, ethical, and moral values will help you sustain.

I urge the new generation to open dialogues with your parents, teachers, and mentors who have been there and done that. Ask about everything that puzzles you without fear of being ridiculed, no matter how basic or illogical the question may seem. Share with them your ideas and the benefits of your wisdom and experience, and above all, your vision of the world. Do not assume the older generation knows about your ways and your world.

My sabbatical liberated me in a lot of ways and helped me rekindle my spirit to be free to think openly without bias and without being constrained by age-old norms. It encouraged me to appreciate the virtue of slowness necessary to fully enjoy life around me, and especially the company of people I love and the relationships I value so much. The hard part is bringing about the change in your life, but once that unknown journey begins, you feel you have entered the land of Shan-gri-la, where everything seems perfect in harmony and your dreams seem very achievable.

The point I am making through the benefit of my experiences and experiments is this: There is not just one way to live life and go about dealing with issues in the most traditional ways. Sometimes one must look for answers outside one's comfort zone and lead the way not travelled often. Each generation should not feel obligated or pressed to follow the same path that their parents followed. When appropriate it would be helpful to draw inspiration from the lives of the previous generation without being burdened with the baggage that attaches to them. Even more important is the fact that within each generation, every individual is built different, physically and emotionally, and it is the responsibility of all generations to recognize that fact and work in a way that makes everyone succeed.

Part III

Human Relationships & Enlightenment

CHAPTER 10
Human Relationships

True love doesn't happen right away; it's an ever-growing process. It develops after you have gone through ups and downs, when you have suffered together, cried together, laughed together.

Richardo Montalban, Actor

I have come to the end in my search for truth to find out what it is in us that brings failure at every stage of our lives in spite of our efforts and what takes us farther away from making our world a better place. All of the above-mentioned things are important: our roles as individuals and collectively as institutions, recognizing our assets and liabilities, understanding nature, and the importance of preserving it, our interconnectedness with one another, recounting the heroic efforts of our leaders, and trying to clear the path to set directions for the future. This quest cannot be completed without recognizing human nature, our inner strengths, and the love and affection that bind us all in many ways and motivates us in the first place, to be good.

The many faces of love and relationships both permanent and transient, initiate and create everything that follows. The human mind, in its mysterious ways, experiences, absorbs, analyzes, and interacts with others to influence and shape lives and to help build comprehensive relationships that guide everything else. Without these connections, we are like those solitary atoms floating in the universe incapable of bonding with others.

I analyzed my own life to see how these forces of love and resulting relationships work and how these relationships have influenced my decisions and actions. I came to the conclusion that no matter how independent you feel to do what you want and to go wherever you want, your deep relationships and your love for others, and their love for you, will always guide you to choose a path that is mutually beneficial in the long run. Therefore, we must always value these relationships and find enough inspiration from them to chart our course in life.

What's this love we all experience at some time or the other, whether or not we talk about it? There is not a soul on this earth who is not a worthy beneficiary of it.

Love and marriage

We all have our love stories to tell, the beginnings of which are often rooted through our parents' unselfish love for us. I experienced my first love some 40 plus years ago, which I think is just beginning to bloom. I met the woman of my dreams at an apartment house in India where our families lived. She was then a teenager bubbling with energy and confidence. Since then, we have been through a lot together, the good, the not so good, victories, defeats, disappointments, mistakes, and milestones, but most of all we have grown together and travelled through time not knowing where our journey would take us. Our love has seen many colors, enameled with passion, care, tears, laughter, smiles, and that mysterious bond, or chemistry if you will, between us held us together for decades. The most fulfilling result of our love, however, is the gift of two beautiful children, a son and daughter, who developed into mature and socially responsible adults.

Let me make one thing very clear: Time alone does not heal everything nor does it teach you everything. There are things about each other, and how we feel about things, we are still figuring out, and in that regard, we are only a work in progress. There are no regrets because we are passing through life's journey together, making adjustments and picking each other up when one is down, onwards and forward, toward perfecting and feeling good about ourselves in the process.

We created our own love story just like millions of lucky couples, and along the way we were inspired by Shakespeare's *Romeo and Juliet, Heer & Ranjha* (an Indian love story), and the American movie classic, *Love Story* among others. That memorable line from *Love Story*, "Love is never having to say you're sorry," still rings in my ears. This makes one understand the true meaning of love when the two individuals relinquish their own existence to give way to the new entity, "us." Love heals everything. It creates miracles. One must believe in it and not lose hope because it takes time for its healing power to work. I am living proof of that.

There is also this issue of marriage, which can be painful and a lot more complicated than falling in love. What is marriage? I define marriage as an agreement between two willing adults to spend their life together as a couple, usually blessed and witnessed by a priest or a judge, and family and friends. On a social note, I must admit I am against elaborate ceremonies and fortunes spent on weddings that for some, create unsustainable financial obligations.

My wife and I were brought up in a semi-conservative society where arranged marriages are common, so for us to get the approval of our parents was a nearly impossible task. Finally, believing in my conviction and steadfastness and my wife, a firm believer in God, we overcame that hurdle and got our parents' blessings. The rest has been nothing short of a wonderful life. To make the record complete, I must thank my dear cousin Uma, the one person without whose efforts I may have lost contact with my sweetheart. Cousin Uma made careful efforts to arrange a reunion between me and my sweetheart at a local farm. We could not thank her enough. That evening has been the most memorable moment of our lives.

For young people contemplating getting seriously involved in relationships, let me remind you in order for those relationships to last, you will need a lot of courage, patience, a sense of sacrifice, which will be tested at every stage and phase of that relationship, and you will have to give everything you have to sustain that relationship in the midst of life's uncertainties. There may be many distractions along the way. More importantly, when you have children, a very testament to your mutual love, you will be called upon to share your life with them. This evolution of parental care and love will be part natural and part deliberate. Love will take a whole new meaning for you and your partner in which the attention will shift outside, to the impact you will make in the lives of others. Your universe will suddenly expand, and more and more people will benefit from your love and the attention you give them. In many ways you will become a mirror image of your parents and will appreciate everything they did for you when you were growing up. Suddenly you will realize all of your life you were the recipient of the most unselfish, caring, and protective love from your parents, which you took for granted. Finally, when you enter the official years of your life, you will understand and appreciate the love abundant in nature, the love of saints and priests who themselves practice a hard and simple life yet show you the way to happiness. Thus the legacy lives on.

Other social and professional relationships

If you are true to yourself and respect others, you will achieve true love for your sake and others, and you will be liked and loved in spite of your inherent limitations as a human being. For any relationship to work, whether personal or professional, the key ingredients are mutual respect and understanding. Along life's journey we make many friends, and some of whom last a lifetime. We learn a lot from those experiences. Having similar backgrounds with some friends can make the ride smooth, while dissimilar upbringings require extra efforts in building and sustaining relationships. We must try to recognize the commonalities among ourselves and respect them to achieve the most out of our relationships. I have been quite lucky in this regard and found true friends and acquaintances, based on mutual respect, despite different interests and beliefs.

Professional contacts require a certain level of diplomacy and sense of purpose for them to work. In the absence of a contract, the objective criteria as to the expectations must be met. Simply put, the objective criteria is how a prudent person would act in a similar set of circumstances. Personal and business relationships must be kept separate to avoid conflicts of interest and expectations. I have witnessed really good friendships jeopardized in the wake of business disputes. It takes a long time to repair them, and most never return to their pre-dispute stage. Relationships are delicate. They take years to build, but can be ruined in a second due to a trivial misunderstanding and self-interest.

The role of women

One cannot appreciate enough the role women

play in creating, maintaining, and furthering relationships as well as the nurturing, care, and protection they provide. Women often do this with just the right amount of love to make all relationships work. Therefore, I admit my wife has a better success rate than I have in resolving disputes regarding our telephone, cable, or health bills. Throughout my life I have been blessed with enough love and attention from my mom, grandmothers, grand aunts, aunts, sister, cousins, friends, neighbors, teachers, and most of all, from my sweetheart. I have argued with my wife many times on many human and social issues, or in dealing with our children. In the end, though, my objective criteria and logical thinking theory almost always fail, and I am left feeling like a fool. Often I failed to recognize her power of love and her keen sense of human feelings.

Although men have come a long way culturally and politically in recognizing women as their equals, there is still work to be done. There continues to exist social and corporate cultures that discriminate against women, both in their behavior toward women and in compensating them. Equal pay for equal work is still far from universally being implemented. Many cases of sexual discrimination and harassment do not get reported. Therefore, the data claiming improvements do not reflect a true and complete picture. Men need to clean up their act and work together with women to make real progress. Spiritually, if men followed the path of love and nonviolence that come naturally to women and see the world through that prism, all the world's problems would be solved faster. I find women to be more religious than men. Their beliefs seem to give them more inner strength to deal with tragedies and failures. In my experience, women's quotient of tolerance is higher than that of men. Women build around them the environment of trust and comfort, which makes you feel secure and helps you build your character. If you are seeking God and the Ultimate Truth, you will find women to be the perfect gatekeepers to God's kingdom.

Chapter 11
Enlightenment

The true value of a human being is determined primarily by the measure and the sense in which he has attained liberation from the self.

Albert Einstein

On seeking God, or truth, or inner peace

As mentioned in the preceding chapter, being in a meaningful relationship with a woman, in my opinion, will bring you a step closer to achieving the ultimate truth, salvation, and peace within, and with the world. However, I am not an expert on understanding all kinds of relationships between human beings and arguments can be made about them. This is more so in a world that is ever changing where people are reaching new heights in emotional maturity and people with traditional values have come to respect, understand, and honor the choices their fellow citizens make. In the end, what is most important: A ground is made for all relationships to take root, grow, and flourish.

I am not a regular visitor to temples. I do not practice any ritual recommended either by a priest or family, nor am I attached to any particular religion or sect. Each summer my wife and I drive 120 miles to a temple she has grown attached to because she strongly feels her faith in and devotion to Lord Krishna has brought a lot of good in her life. My faith in Godly powers comes from seeing the inherent good in others and by respecting and understanding the natural forces that control our lives. I respect other people's choices as to their beliefs and customs. Having learned a little about the lives of Christ and Buddha, I developed a fair amount of respect and love for them and, therefore, strongly feel if we practiced our lives and our dealings based on their teachings, we will find truth, peace, and the true meaning of our existence. Oliver Joan Duncan Oliver's book, *Coffee with The Buddha*, spells out the four noble truths pronounced by Buddha after he achieved enlightenment:

- Life is suffering.
- The cause of suffering is desire or attachment.
- Non-attachment is possible.
- The middle way-shunning the extremes of asceticism and indulgence-is the path to non-attachment.

Life as we know it is full of desire and attachment, which cause suffering when not fulfilled. Our conscious efforts to move to the middle enable us to achieve coexistence with other people and species. This state ultimately leads us to the highest spiritual state in which our mind, soul, and body are free from desires and possessions. This state of non-attachment is called asceticism. In this ultimate state, one finds peace with oneself, with the surrounding world, and with God.

If we all believed in the profoundness of this thought, and lived our lives accordingly, we would not have created this crisis, or all the other conflicts caused by our differences and our desire to protect the narrow interests and borders, which we arbitrarily created. If we lived our lives in the true spirit of non-attachment, our color, languages, religions, and national affiliations would not separate us from one another, because we would have the wisdom to embrace everyone in spite of those differences. In addition, we would protect the environment, not waste its vast resources and not acquire them only for a competitive edge. In the absence of desire to accumulate and amass wealth, there would be no temptation to cheat, steal, or manipulate because the resources would be there for everyone's benefit.

Buddha understood not everyone can reach the highest spiritual state; therefore, he offered a middle way. The world's problems can be solved in that middle way with peaceful coexistence by everyone sacrificing a little bit. One then may individually proceed toward attaining total non-attachment, when one's task is done on this earth.

This brings me to the inevitable question of death—a journey unknown, beyond anyone's comprehension.

Death and eulogy

Everyone knows they will face the inevitable end one day, but no one wants to talk about it. At some point we have all experienced the loss of loved ones and of those we were not so close. Personally I have lost a lot of relatives, but when I lost my father first and my mom a few years ago, it made me feel so helpless. I felt like an orphan. Age does not make a difference when it comes to feeling your parents' love for you. All of a sudden, upon their death, you feel robbed of that love that made everything else easy. Time rarely heals these deep wounds, but it gives you strength to deal with the pain and sorrow. You eventually come to appreciate the life around you and the world you have created.

When someone passes away, there are tears to shed, times to remember, and words to say. Some have fond memories to share, while some have regrets for not having bonded well with those who have passed away and unabashedly they share that, too. There are also mild complaints aimed at the departed soul, which they did not have the courage to bring up during the life of that person. Often the words are somber celebratory rejoicing moments spent with the departed ones while they were alive, rather than sobbing in sorrow. Life's ordinary moments passed, the memory of which suddenly takes on an extraordinary tone and meaning. If I were, or if we were, or if we didn't, or if we did are the phrases that start pouring at these gatherings. This down to earth experience, although surrounded by sadness, ties everyone together solidly with enough strength to move on.

We can change our lives through this experience if we bring this spirit of harmony and goodness of that moment in our daily lives. If only we love one another and lend a shoulder for people to rest on, at the same time truly try and understand people's innermost feelings and fulfill them to the extent possible, we will have created a better world. If only we were honest with those around us to clear any misunderstandings and take corrective action, it would benefit all immensely. If we did all this, then we will all have lived our lives fully, ably, and honorably, and there won't be any regrets and no ifs at the funerals of our beloveds. We will only have good and happy memories to feel and share.

♦♦♦

It has been a total joy sharing my views and experiences. This may open up the doors through which communication can flow freely for mutual benefit, and create new relationships where we could learn from one another so new ideas and points of view will evolve in the process. With the beautiful opening ceremonies of the 2014 Winter Olympics in Sochi, Russia, still fresh in our minds and souls, let us pledge to bring peace, harmony, and prosperity to all humankind.

God bless.

Epilogue

It is not the strongest of the species that survives, nor the most intelligent, but the one most responsive to change.

Charles Darwin

During my efforts compiling this book and after its completion, I had the privilege to meet with many people. Some I have known intimately, some professionally, some casual acquaintances, and others were total strangers. I was able to discuss with them the issues put forth in the book. Hence, this chapter is dedicated to all those I came in contact with during the past four to five years who share my same concerns, but also have their own stories of how they were affected by the financial crisis of circa 2008, how they dealt with it, how their lives have been shaped by others, and how they were able to contribute positively in shaping the lives of other people around them, as well as their views on economy, globalization, and social values. This book would not be complete without recounting those views. I continue to pick up stories as they unfold daily, as well as continue to study the current state of the economy.

The crisis and its aftermath altered the lives of millions of people around the globe in a profound way. Although we are on a path to recovery, the rate of growth has been less than satisfactory. The unemployment rate in the United States, for instance, which was around 10% in the initial year of the crisis has been steady between 6% and 7% in

2013 and the first half of 2014. The fate of those 50 years old and older, especially those who have been out of work for over 6 months, does not look promising as many in this age group are finding it difficult to reenter the workforce. Some returned to school to beef up their profiles in the hope of making themselves more marketable. This crisis has forced many to work multiple jobs in order to honor their daily commitments. Many people have lost their homes, mostly to foreclosures, and are scrambling to find cheap or affordable rental options. Due to a lack of a sustainable job or paid internship, graduates have moved back home with their parents. These young Americans seem to be in a permanent holding pattern with respect to their plans to start families and realize the American dream. Those who have held onto their jobs during the crisis and those lucky few who found new jobs for the most part are overworked and under-appreciated. In some cases, their hours have been curtailed significantly, while many in the process now have reduced benefits for lack of eligibility. Many at the lower end of the workforce have not seen raises in their compensation since the crisis began in 2008, yet prices for essentials continue to creep up above the inflation rate to make it even harder for common folks to survive. It boggles my mind to see those in the financial sector who, year after year, continue to enjoy multi-million dollar year-end bonuses.

Worldwide the story remains the same as

recently noted by *Swiss News*. According to the study, some 202 million people are currently jobless, and that number is likely to reach 215 million if the current climate continues. Of those 202 million unlucky people, approximately 75 million are in the 15 to 24 age group, which brings the world-wide youth unemployment rate to an unconscionable 13%. In Spain, the rate in that category is 57%. Rightly so, Carl Bildt, Swiss Foreign Minister, considers the youth unemployment as a "cancer on society." In a similar study they also found the world's 85 richest people have the same wealth as half the world's population. Obviously, in spite of all the efforts in the last four to five years to restore stability and growth in the world economy and bring millions out of poverty, in fact, we are headed in the wrong direction.

Yet there is hope if we take notice of the unusual profile of Sam Polk, a former hedge-fund trader and founder of the nonprofit Groceryships, chronicled in *The New York Times Sunday Review* on January 19, 2014. He said he had not been hooked on alcohol or drugs, but on money. He later transformed himself by taking a small step in the right direction by helping people who actually need the money, and in the process made a real contribution to the world. Some of those who were surrounded by wealth all their life are beginning to get a sense of how much is enough when they realize a few extra millions do not make a tangible difference in their lives. Consulting companies such as McKinsey, after a culture crisis at the top for some time, are trying to regain the confidence and trust of their clients and people under the new leadership, setting a much needed ethical tone at the top. This is done by increasing the transparency at all levels of the organization and creating a culture that has zero tolerance for unethical behavior.

Even average people from Main Street are beginning to appreciate and evaluate their role in the aftermath and connect the dots, such as Cynthia Yoder who revealed this in the context of what we have all gone though:

> *The most difficult thing for me during the crisis was seeing so many people suffer and not feeling any sense of power to do anything about it. After some soul-searching, I understood my role in helping the financial recovery was to continue my work and continue our household practice of charitable giving. I am a spiritual mentor and a writing mentor, helping people live purposeful lives through self-expression. The crisis heightened for me that when you are living "on purpose" then you can easily find meaning. You tend to turn less to materialism to fulfill your needs and more toward an inner compass. The crisis, in my view, was a course correction after rampant materialism and greed ruled the day. I hope that we have learned the lessons, so that we can move forward with greater compassion for each other and the planet and less focused on getting the biggest*

piece of the pie.

I am sure many share her feelings and are willing to contribute their fair share so that we can remain *whole.*

What is happening in the financial world? Big banks continue to pay billions of dollars in penalties settling the lawsuits emanating from investigations into lack of oversight and accountability during the crisis as well as financial scandals. Yet there is increased opposition to new regulatory laws, especially the much contested Volker rule, which was included in the law to restrict the trading and investing activities of the financial institutions for their own account. The IMF thinks the big banks still pose a threat to the world financial system because there is an assumption that governments will rescue them in case of trouble. Some European countries, such as Iceland, refused to offer bailouts to banks there and instead broke them up into more manageable domestically viable and sustainable entities. One of the measures taken to stop the bleeding was to fire the old executives and cap bonuses to a reasonable 25% of regular compensation.

In the United States there appears to be some silver lining on the otherwise bleak economic prospects of millions of hard-working, struggling Americans. The President signed an executive order in 2013 to increase the minimum wage from $7.25 to $10.10 per hour. The bill hasn't passed yet. In the meanwhile, 14 states raised the minimum wage in varying degree effective January 2014, and more states are expected to follow. In a recent poll conducted from December 12 to 15, 2013, by the Washington Post-ABC News, about two in three Americans are in favor of increasing the minimum wage. 57% of Americans also believe the government should pursue policies at balancing an economic system by combating inequality. The nation's leading economists also favor this view. I could not agree more. As far as the demand of fast food and retail workers, supported by FFF, to increase the minimum wage up to $15, it will take careful negotiation and not just hunger strikes to resolve the issue because there are some serious considerations as to increased costs and even possibilities of shutdowns of small establishments.

In his last State of the Union address, President Barack Obama proposed the creation of small MyRA savings accounts for those people not covered by employer sponsored 401-K plans. The MyRA that are expected to go into effect in 2015, have a lifetime cap of $15,000, at which point it would have to be transferred to a private sector Roth IRA. The account can be opened with $25 and contributions can be made into it for as little as $5. There are no fees to maintain these accounts and the investments are considered safer than privately managed high-return high-risk investments.

Meanwhile, who is listening to the cries of the jobless and homeless? From December 9 to 13, 2013, *The New York Times* wrote a five-part story about Dasani, an aspiring young girl living in a homeless shelter with her family. These eye-opening stories tell how fortunate most of us are compared to people living in subhuman conditions only a few blocks away from affluent upper middle class people. There are pets in suburbia and high-rises living better lives than these unfortunate people. If something is not done immediately for the 22,000 or so homeless children in New York City and many more across the country, then there isn't much hope left for our future. Something needs to get done and fast before the abandoned youth lose their patience and their ability to succeed because they are in a trap. We will all be responsible if we cannot turn these budding youth into valuable assets of the society and instead let them become our liability.

♦♦♦

As a civilized society, it is our social and moral obligation to bring sustainable recovery to all the segments of the world population. In that joint process, with the respective governments and civilians working side by side, we may be tempted to look at past successes and apply the old theories that worked in the past and expect them to work again this time. In reality, though, the answer may lie in departing from the beaten path and finding new ways by nurturing fresh ideas, appreciating and learning from nature and the natural forces surrounding us, being united in all our efforts, and shifting the focus outward, thereby preserving and creating true physical assets as well as social and moral values. When our next recovery arrives, it must not merely become some statistic for the record books, but must truly be the testimony to our joint efforts in building a sustainable world for everyone.

Acknowledgments

This book would not have seen the light of day without the care, encouragement, advice, suggestions, and support of many whom I am privileged to mention here. In addition, countless articles, books, people, and situations have proved to be a constant source of inspiration for me and helped keep me going and not give up, which there was always a fear of. Thanks to you all.

First, thanks to my late parents Mr. B M Bhatt and Mrs. I B Bhatt who cared for me so much throughout my life and inspired me to do my best no matter what the circumstances were. They showed the way how to live by sharing with others and caring for all who they came in contact with. I picture them smiling with joy right now for my efforts. This book is dedicated to them for their *first class* contribution to the community in spite of their own middle class struggles.

My love and thanks to Niranjana, my wife, who has shown remarkable patience not just during my time writing this book but throughout our 40 plus years of association. I am just so damn lucky to have found a soul mate like her. To my children, Milan and Garima, who just by being the socially responsible and lovable individuals they are, make my every waking moment and every breath worthwhile.

Special thanks to Bharat, my brother, who has had a phenomenal career as a banker, who was my role model when I was growing up, and who insisted I should come to America and build my career here. After initial hesitation, I did just that eventually. I am deeply indebted to him because he showed me the way, and I thank his wife, Rupa, who has been always supportive of his decisions. I have been blessed with the love, care, and guidance which I received unconditionally from my sister, Maya, and with her husband, Kersi, both graduates in literature, and my brother, Pradip, who is a practicing chartered accountant in India, for his guidance and support and a constant source of inspiration (also my speechwriter for my high school elocution competitions), and his wife, Bharati, supporting him every step of the way and for tirelessly taking care of our parents throughout, but especially during their terminal years.

As I mentioned earlier I had a very happy childhood and was blessed to have received unconditional love and affection from my many aunts, uncles, grandparents, grand uncles, grand aunts, dozens of cousins from either side, neighbors, friends, teachers, and even strangers who all have in some form or shape contributed to my success and my being a useful member of the society. I thank them all for their love and care and guidance. It also makes me very happy and satisfied to see our children, and our nieces and nephews, get along so well; they all have succeeded well and are beginning to build their nests of hope and a sustainable future.

My special thanks to those who took great care in going through the manuscript, so it would have a shot at becoming a real book. Thanks to Patrick Irish, a young professional and a Millennial, for going through the first draft in one sitting and making helpful comments along the way. Thanks for sharing your perspectives. To Kersi Mistry, my sister's husband and an able advisor in this effort, your painstaking efforts and your helpful suggestions as to diction and form helped me refine the bulk of my writing here and for that I am deeply thankful. To Cynthia Yoder, my friend and business associate, I appreciate your valuable comments, which I took in advisement in restructuring the format and rearranging the script so that it narrates smoothly and in logical sequence without undermining the central theme of the book. I also appreciate you sharing your thoughts on the crisis and how you dealt with the aftermath. It meant a lot to me. To my train buddy, Walter Frank, who in spite of his busy schedule and in the midst of his own writing projects, found time to carefully go through the manuscript and offer honest suggestions, many thanks. My heartfelt thanks to my fellow professional Joseph Salvatore with whom I have spent many moments reflecting on our views of the world, I very much appreciate the care he offered in going through the manuscript. Thanks for listening, man. Thanks to Julia Sass Rubin for blessing this project and finding time in spite of her overwhelming schedule educating others and promoting changes and improvement in school education. None of this would have been possible without the painstaking efforts by my publisher Karen Hodges Miller of Open Door Publishing in taking on this project and Jacquelyn Pillsbury who proofread the entire script with unequalled dedication and their patience in bringing the original script, which was a bit rough around the edges to say the least, to its ultimate fruition.

Public accounting has taught me a lot. It has helped me be more efficient, alert, and well-rounded in many areas of business. It has helped me connect the dots and see things globally. Thanks to my mentors, superiors, colleagues, and associates for the rich experiences and for helping me grow. I could not be who I am today without their support and encouragement I received over the past 40 years or so. They have influenced me in many ways and helped me see things from many perspectives. Having the benefit of being groomed in an open environment throughout, I can say with pride that I have been able to promote and practice what I believe in, all along.

About the Author

Anil B. Bhatt CPA, M Tax, has been in the practice of accounting for over 30 years servicing individuals, businesses, and not-for-profits in the New York metropolitan area.

After spending his working years in Manhattan, he is recently operating a private practice out of Princeton, New Jersey, and a virtual office in New York. While continuing to help clients with their accounting and tax planning and preparation needs, he is seeking out entities who have embedded corporate social responsibility in their DNA. He continues to build alliances with other professionals around this concept.

After he left a full-time job, he took a sabbatical that coincided with the financial crisis of 2008. The events of the financial crisis, its aftermath, and his experiences during his long career in accounting inspired him to write a book chronicling those events and offering a recipe for survival in these uncertain times.

He lives near Princeton, New Jersey, with his wife. They have two children, a son and a daughter, both graduated and now passionately involved in their respective not-for-profit with worthy social causes.